Finding Our Humanity

An inner journey towards understanding
ourselves and our way forward

LEIF COCKS

First Published in 2019 by
The Orangutan Project

National Library of Australia Cataloguing-in-Publication data:

ISBN-13: 978-0-6485018-0-0 (paperback edition)
ISBN-13: 978-0-6485018-1-7 (e book)

Cover graphic design by Celeste Njoo for The Orangutan Project

All profits from the sale of this book will go towards orangutan conservation projects to ensure orangutans' survival in the wild.

Printed by EnviroPrint Australia on 100% recycled post consumer waste paper made carbon neutral.

Also by Leif Cocks:

Orangutans My Cousins, My Friends:
A journey to understand and save the person of the forest

Orangutans and Their Battle for Survival

Dedication

I dedicate this book to all orangutans.
May it be that one day you will all live safe and free.

Acknowledgements

I would like to acknowledge all those who have shared, and continue to share, my journey to save orangutans and make a better world for all living beings.

In particular, I am grateful to The Orangutan Project's board, staff, contractors, volunteers and donors. You are my inspiration and my friends. Thank you.

I would also like to thank, Jennifer Marr, for helping me to share the story of my friends, the orangutans, and in doing so, to speak up for those who cannot speak for themselves.

Contents

Foreword

With rates of depression and anxiety soaring in the Western world, our insatiable hunger for possessions, growth and instant information has brought with it, emotional starvation. We are connected globally at the touch of a button through a multitude of forums. Yet never have so many of us felt more disconnected, without purpose and alone.

As the impact of the human population on our environment continues to grow, countless other species that also inhabit our Earth, are pushed closer to extinction. For many, that sentence has already been inflicted. Sadly, the orangutan, one of our closest living relatives, is on the precipice of extinction as it faces unprecedented pressures from habitat destruction and poaching.

But this is not a story of despair. Leif's book, '*Finding our Humanity*', is a story of hope and inspiration. Having worked closely with Leif and orangutans for half of my life, Leif has been a constant presence during my adulthood. I will always be grateful that he chose to pass the torch to me to care for the precious orangutans or 'orange kids' as we affectionately call them at Perth Zoo. That moment in time really was the beginning of my journey to find my own humanity. I grew an unyielding and fiery passion to speak for and protect this truly beautiful, intelligent and sentient species that had no voice of its own in this world, despite sharing 97% of our human DNA.

Leif has been an inspiration to me and many others. His commitment to orangutan conservation is steadfast and unwavering and he leads with integrity and wisdom. His knowledge on human behaviour has contributed to The Orangutan Project developing into a highly effective organisation that is having a very real impact on orangutan conservation and welfare. His clarity of mind and the ability to make decisions both with his head and heart are vital attributes when dealing with complex conservation issues in developing countries.

The word 'orangutan' literally translates to 'person of the forest.' In '*Finding our Humanity*', Leif calls on us to discover and extend our humanity to all living beings and to appreciate their value and right to live safe, wild and free.

We are placed in a pivotal point in time to save the orangutan. By searching within ourselves and then coming together with a common purpose as a group, we have a remarkable opportunity to harness our humanity to save our beloved orange cousins.

Time is ticking. Will you join us?

Kylie Bullo
Conservation Project Manager- The Orangutan Project

Prologue

'What you seek is seeking you.'
Rumi

The spark of humanity resides within all of us. We each have it, yet differences lie in what we understand humanity to be. For some, it is defined by our biology alone, the physical characteristics which make us human. For others it is evidenced by our behaviours, cultural beliefs, language and innate human nature. Whilst others still regard it as best demonstrated in acts of compassion, empathy, kindness and generosity of spirit of which we are all capable. For me, the definition of humanity encompasses all of these and more. Expanding beyond the borders of our traditional understanding and into wider realms of possibility which beckon to us all if we can open our hearts and minds to experience it.

Interestingly my journey to reach this understanding did not occur in a blinding flash nor in a single revelatory moment. Instead it has been formed over a lifetime of moments. More as a process of learning and gentle evolution within, as life offered me the situations and circumstances, people and events which would guide me along the path. This included the opportunity to interact with and work for orangutans, for it is these beings I have come to know and love. This is why I have dedicated my life's work to their protection and survival. It has been my experiences with these unique beings which has most informed and shaped my sense of what true humanity is and can be. I trust that this may be the case for you too as you read this book.

Yet I do not expect or direct you to follow my path. Rather my intention is to explain how I came to this point and share the profound benefits I have witnessed both within my own life and the lives of others, when this way of being is embraced. In doing so, I hope you can likewise gain from the lessons life has taught me.

I also think it is worthwhile to point out that as a biologist, conservationist and orangutan specialist with a keen interest in philosophy the book that you hold in your hands is written from this perspective. Therefore the stories and insights are drawn from my professional fields of expertise, the personal interactions I have shared with orangutans, chimpanzees and other members of the great ape family as well as my own inner journey. It is these which have most influenced my way of being in the world and my particular lived experiences. With this in mind I hope you will enjoy some of the unique encounters I have had and what I have learned from these.

Perhaps most importantly, my hope is that a shift in the way we see ourselves, our place in the world and our *humanity* itself will assist us to make the changes required on the planet today - not just for our own survival, but for that of all living beings. Now more than ever it is time that we let go of our past ways of being, our outdated perceptions and move to a more holistic, compassionate approach to life. An approach which supports and benefits us all, now and into the future. This is because I know what is possible when good people work towards a common cause for the best outcome for all living beings. It is here that major steps forward can be taken and valuable long term results achieved in conservation and animal welfare. This is what The Orangutan Project and its sister organisations, International Elephant Project and International Tiger Project, have been working for and will continue to do so until the survival of our orange cousins and other wild beings has been assured.

Introduction

*'We cannot despair of humanity, since we
ourselves are human beings.'*
Albert Einstein

The Tale of the Tapanuli

In a little known corner of northern Sumatra in the South East Asian archipelago of Indonesia an astonishing scientific discovery was made by primatologists when they began to study an isolated group of orangutans in around 2005.[1] Previously assumed to be Sumatran orangutans, researchers found that this theory was incorrect. By 2017 scientists announced the exciting news that another distinct species of great ape had been discovered. This newly identified member of the Hominid family being the orangutans from this remote region of the island. Aptly named the Tapanuli orangutan or Pongo tapanuliensis, after the Tapanuli area in which they live, the population was found in the rugged highland forests of the Batang Toru Ecosystem in the region south of Lake Toba. [2]

With the addition of these unique beings the great ape family swelled to eight distinct species. These now include the Tapanuli, Bornean and Sumatran orangutans, common chimpanzee, bonobo or pygmy chimpanzee, the Eastern and Western gorillas and, of course, humans. Not since the comparative genome sequencing of all the great apes less than two decades ago, had primatologists shared such ground breaking information for the Hominid family. A new twenty first century great ape had been discovered, one which had existed unacknowledged by humans for tens of thousands of years.

Unsurprisingly, global communities of primatologists and conservationists celebrated the rare find as evidence of the wonder and diversity of the natural world. A world which obviously still holds many fascinating secrets for us to uncover. Furthermore, with the discovery of the Tapanuli orangutan, researchers were able to piece together a better picture of the evolutionary journey of each of the different orangutan species. According to archaeological evidence, orangutans first arrived on the islands of Sumatra, Borneo and Java after travelling down from Asia millions of years ago, during an earlier ice age. At various times in the past these islands had been connected to the mainland and each other via land bridges that existed at a time of lower sea levels.

It then appears that around 3.38 million years ago, the Sumatran orangutans north of Lake Toba were separated from their Tapanuli and Bornean relatives. Later, as the planet warmed and sea levels rose, the land bridges between Sumatra, Borneo and Java disappeared. This meant that the Tapanuli and Bornean orangutans became separated from each other around 670,000 years ago. [3] Interestingly, genome sequencing of the three species has shown that mitochondrial DNA is more alike between the Tapanuli and Bornean species. However, the nuclear DNA is more closely aligned between the Sumatran and Tapanuli orangutans.[4] As such, their unique genome reveals some answers to questions about the divergent ancestral history of the three species. Intriguingly, it seems that the Tapanuli is perhaps the most ancient of the three lineages of orangutan. [5]

Differing from their Bornean and Sumatran relatives in a number of significant ways, the Tapanuli represent a distinct and separate evolutionary path demonstrating specific adaptations to their secluded environment. Physically, the Tapanuli has thicker, light reddish brown coloured hair with a coarse, if not frizzy texture. In terms of facial hair, adult males possess a definite moustache with beard as well as less pronounced, flatter cheek flanges, whilst the females also have beards. [6] Their skulls and jawbones are smaller and their molar teeth also differ from those of other orangutans.[7] In terms of diet, the Tapanuli displays a preference for a range of plants, fruits and flowers not known to be consumed by the other orangutan species. They are also willing to eat caterpillars and cones from conifer trees.[8] The characteristic *long call*, which is sent out into the forest by adult males for both territorial and mating purposes, is also distinctly different amongst the Tapanuli orangutans. The Tapanuli live in habitats which range from lowland riverine areas up to more rugged highland regions which are around 850m above sea level, demonstrating they are uniquely adapted to their environment.[9]

However, like their Sumatran and Bornean relatives, Tapanuli orangutans are intelligent, sentient beings. As arboreal great apes, they live within semi-solitary social structures in their tree top habitat. They display tool use as well as a highly developed cultural knowledge which makes them well equipped to navigate life in the dense rainforests in which they live. This cultural knowledge covers information on over 2,000 edible food sources, seasonal fruiting, nest building, communication, social interaction and avoidance of predators. This is passed down from mothers to their young during their eight to nine year period of intensive maternal care.

The female Tapanuli's reproductive cycle is similar to that of the Sumatran orangutan. Females mature sexually at around 15 years of age with a birth interval of between eight to nine years in length, due to the long term raising of their offspring. Females also remain fertile for their life span of up to 50 to 60 years of age and will seek out a nearby dominant male when they are in oestrus and ready to mate. Also, like all other great apes, Tapanuli orangutans have a gestation period of around eight and a half to nine months, usually giving birth to one offspring at a time. The birth of twins or multiple newborns is the exception rather than the norm and occurs at about the same rate as in humans. Unfortunately, the Tapanuli's distinctive reproductive cycle means that they are exceptionally slow to reproduce. The result of this being that the loss of only a relatively small percentage of mature females within a population can expose them to the risk of extinction. However, their discovery demonstrated that, against great odds, the Tapanuli has hung on to survival in a number of separately clustered populations of the region.

Yet celebrations at the identification of the new species were short lived. By 2018, the Tapanuli orangutan was pronounced the rarest and most endangered great ape in the world. With an estimated number of only 800 of these remarkable orangutans remaining in the wild, the Tapanuli is now even more threatened with extinction than its relatives, the Sumatran and Bornean orangutans. Almost to mark the occasion, the Tapanuli orangutan was included as *Critically Endangered (CR)* on the International Union for Conservation of Nature's (IUCN) Red List in 2018.[10] A list which offers the world's most comprehensive inventory of threatened animal and plant species as well as those in imminent danger of extinction.

Importantly, it wasn't just the low population numbers of this species which warranted their inclusion as Critically Endangered on the Red List. Their isolated habitat within the Batang Toru Ecosystem is also under the looming threat of destruction. Not only are logging and gold mining currently permitted within some parts of the fragile environment, it has been confirmed that a Chinese hydro-electric dam is planned for construction right in the middle of the ecosystem. The creation of this dam would not only flood key sections of the orangutan's habitat, it would most certainly consign the newly discovered species to rapid extinction. Difficult to believe, but unfortunately true, this devastating news confirmed the impending extermination of the newest addition to our great ape family, the Tapanuli orangutan.

As word spread of the plight of the Tapanuli, many around the globe asked, *"How could this occur and in such a brief period of time?"* As an orangutan specialist and conservation advocate for all three species of orangutan, the answers for me were clear and based upon a number of cumulative effects. Firstly, as already mentioned the Tapanuli's long reproductive cycle and cultural adaptations of intensive child raising periods set the stage for them being highly susceptible to extinction, especially if the number of reproductive females declines. Secondly, with the combined impacts of population loss from wholesale slaughter, hunting, poaching for the illegal pet trade, logging, mining, invasive, consistent habitat destruction and large scale development in key orangutan natural environments, it is easy to predict the likely outcome for the Tapanuli.

Sadly their very existence has been pushed to the tipping point and in some quarters there appears to be a marked disregard for the consequences. Unless these impacts can be addressed now, the Tapanuli orangutan will disappear altogether from its last remaining home on the planet. Meaning that this unique species, which has survived and evolved for millions of years, will become extinct in a very short space of time. Furthermore, their extinction will have the tell-tale signature of human activity written all over it because without a doubt the major driving force behind the rapid loss of the Tapanuli population is *us*.

If we can take anything positive out of this story, and I believe we can, the simple truth is that it doesn't have to be this way. We, as humans, can choose to protect and save the Tapanuli orangutan and retain its habitat. However, to do this will require a significant shift in the way we address the issues currently at play. Critically that shift must happen quickly as there is no time to lose for the Tapanuli orangutans. The survival of this species comes down to whether we have the *will to make it happen*, because we certainly have the ability and the means. The choice is up to us and I know we can make the difference in the long term for the survival of these intelligent and aware beings.

The question here is whether we are willing to make the changes required?

A Bigger Picture

*'I think sometimes we need to take a step back and just remember
we have no greater right to be here than any other animal.'*
Sir David Attenborough

There is a larger perspective to consider. Significantly, this perspective is one which not only concerns the survival of other species across the planet, but perhaps ours too. Unfortunately, the precarious position of the Tapanuli orangutan is neither a unique nor an isolated case. Instead, the inconvenient truth is their story can be seen as a microcosm of what is happening around the world today. Predominantly due to the combined effects of human activity, including ongoing habitat destruction in both land and aquatic environments and changes in climate, there are more than 26,500 species currently listed as threatened with extinction on the Red List. [11] Obviously, modern day humans are nowhere to be seen on this list, yet our impact on the planet is clear to see.

Currently the numbers of threatened flora and fauna species are growing and include the following proportions of identified species: *"40% of amphibians, 34% of conifers, 33% of reef building corals, 25% of mammals and 14% of birds."* [12] To underscore these challenging statistics, scientists calculate that, due to the presence of human beings on the planet, global extinction rates are at least 1,000 to 10,000 times higher than would have otherwise occurred. [13] This is especially so as our unsustainable exploitation of resources continues to grow. Furthermore, if the current wave of destruction of the natural world and its living diversity continues, we could well witness what has been termed as 'the sixth extinction.' An era described as potentially being the next major mass extinction in Earth's history and we would collectively shoulder the responsibility for triggering this event. [14]

To put this into perspective regarding the species currently on the planet, a recent study into the estimated bio mass of all living beings on Earth has uncovered some staggering results. The study presented in the *Proceedings of the National Academy of Sciences (PNAS)* was based on a census which measured the estimated bio mass weight of all life by category of biological classification.[15] To carry out this comparative research the unit of measurement specified for each category in the study was gigatons of carbon, which equates to the following:

- One gigaton = one billion metric tons
- One metric ton = 1,000 kilograms.

With the researchers finding an estimated combined weight of approximately 550 gigatons of total carbon bio mass on the planet. From the statistics produced in the study it was clear to see that the life form by category with the most mass was the Plant Kingdom -weighing in at an amazing 450 gigatons. However, looking at the results for members of the Animal Kingdom, the figures become particularly telling. The most sobering results being the comparative weight of agricultural mammal livestock at 0.1 gigatons, the total bio mass of human kind at 0.06 gigatons and remaining wild mammals coming in at 0.007 gigatons. Whilst populations of surviving wild birds weighed in at a diminutive 0.002 gigatons. [16] From these results it is clear that humans, as only a relatively small proportion of all living bio mass, have had and continue to have a marked impact on both the diversity and size of populations of other mammals and wildlife on Earth.

On the one hand, we have hyper-inflated the numbers of a select group of domesticated and food-based species in the form of agricultural livestock. Whilst at the same time our actions have resulted in the decimation of wild mammal populations. I think the infographic below illustrating the relative proportions of 'Bio Mass of all the Land Mammals on Earth' provides an exceptionally clear representation of the effect we are creating. [17]

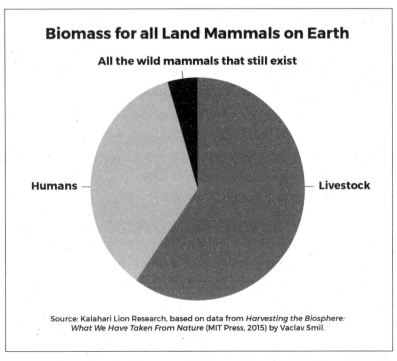

Biomass for all Land Mammals on Earth

All the wild mammals that still exist

Humans — — Livestock

Source: Kalahari Lion Research, based on data from *Harvesting the Biosphere: What We Have Taken From Nature* (MIT Press, 2015) by Vaclav Smil.

We have artificially expanded population numbers of some agricultural livestock species such as cattle, sheep and pigs into the billions. In regards to the poultry industry, it is estimated that around 50 billion chickens are slaughtered each year for human consumption.[18] Whilst other species such as Bornean and Sumatran orangutans, Asian elephants and eastern lowland gorillas are perhaps numbered in their thousands. Some species such as the Tapanuli orangutan are dwindling to the hundreds and there are estimated to be as few as 90 to 120 Javan rhinoceroses remaining in the wild. With these troubling statistics, it is evident that change must occur at a foundational level if we are to retain many of our wild species into the future. Furthermore, in recent times, climate scientists have been questioning whether we will inflict so much damage on the global environment that we will irreparably change the climate of Earth. Perhaps precipitating our own extinction in the not too distant future?

However, much like the story of the Tapanuli orangutan, there are alternative choices we can make and we don't have to continue in this way. On the contrary, over the years I have seen what is possible when we commit to a new and more compassionate course of action. Especially when we work together with a common vision to enact change for the better, not just for ourselves, but for all species with which we share our home planet. Yet it is also clear that we cannot address and solve the issues of today using the same approaches which have created these problems to begin with. To do so would only result in more of the same and serve to support the existing patterns already in operation. Which evidence seems to suggest is placing both human survival and that of all other species at risk. Therefore, instead of continuing with our current trajectory, we need a fresh perspective and a clear commitment to change the way we see, think and act in the world. As to me, humanity is always best evidenced by our ability and willingness to change our point of view, our thinking and our actions when new information comes to light.

This shift in perspective translates into the following key steps:

- *Seeing* – Shifting how we view ourselves and our place amongst all other living beings. We create this change by deepening our understanding of what it is to be human as members of the Animal Kingdom. Firstly broadening our appreciation of our closest great ape relatives and gaining insight into our own behaviours as biological, instinctive, culture based animals, who are also self-aware beings.
- *Thinking* – Firstly, looking within ourselves to seek more balanced solutions and using both our hearts and minds to approach

current issues with a new way of thinking. We achieve this by combining a willingness to let go of our long held assumptions with an openness to learn new ideas, by blending the compassion of the heart with the intellect of the mind. Also utilising creative thinking as well as reasoned logic to address and resolve challenges into the future.

- *Acting* – Taking informed, intelligent, compassionate and solution-based action, with cooperation and collaboration as our aims rather than competition and aggression. As well as being able to think beyond the current imbalances between our masculine and feminine natures, integrating each of these into how we think about the planet. We do this by expanding our way of being in the world to focus on conserving, protecting and valuing all life forms and the planet we call home.

By following this three part approach I trust that we can extend the scope of that which we respect, treasure and safeguard across the planet for the long term. In the case of Critically Endangered orangutans this has been the aim of The Orangutan Project for many years and will continue to be so for as long as is required. As I firmly believe it is vital we redefine and expand our understanding of who we are as humans and what we view as humanity if we are to survive as a species. Just as importantly, grant all other living beings on the planet the opportunity to do the same. Ultimately, it is the collective decisions we make and the actions we take today which will reflect not only who we are as a species but also set the course for who we wish to be in the future.

Perhaps it's time we found our humanity?

Section One
How We See

How we view ourselves as humans and what we understand our humanity to be is governed by our perception, or literally, *how we see*. Yet how we see is deeply influenced by our biological drives, instinctive behaviours, tribal past and cultural beliefs, many of which are outside the scope of our conscious awareness. This makes them not only difficult to identify but often invisible in our field of vision. This is why an exploration of how we perceive the world is vital, as perhaps we are not seeing the full picture in front of us? However, there is another way of seeing, which enables us to be aware of these influences and, therefore, develop a broader, more balanced outlook. To reach this vantage point we must first examine our unquestioned assumptions and consider the contradictions which lie hidden within them. We cannot overcome perceptions, drives and instincts which are not within our consciousness. It is by bringing them into our consciousness, we can recognise and ultimately transcend their influence within our lives. Thus creating a shift in the way we see and opening us up to a greater understanding of the vast possibilities for humankind.

Chapter One
Seeing the Great Ape
in the Room

*'Look deep into nature and then you will
understand everything better'*
Albert Einstein

Defined by Our Biology?

Biologically speaking, you and I belong to the species *Homo
sapiens* and are members of the great ape family. Nestled within the
Animal Kingdom and as part of the web of life on planet Earth, our
full taxonomic classification is as follows:

Domain: *Eukarya,* Kingdom: *Animalia,*
Phylum: *Chordata,*
Class: *Mammalia,*
Order: *Primate*
Family: *Hominidae,* great ape family of *Hominids,*
Genus: *Homo,*
Species: *Sapiens.*

Interestingly our unique species name, *Homo sapiens,* originally
translates from Latin as *Homo* (man or human being) and *sapiens*
(be wise). [19] Which means that we have bestowed upon ourselves

the mantle of the 'wise human.' As such we belong to the biological collective of human beings which make up humanity and it has been our biology by which we have most commonly defined ourselves.

We are also the last remaining members of the genus *Homo* (human) found on the planet, with palaeontologists now estimating that our distinct species first appeared on Earth only around 250,000 to 315,000 years ago. [20] Our closest human relatives, the Neanderthals (*Homo neanderthalensis)* and the Denisovians (*Homo denisova)* became extinct within perhaps the last 40,000 to 50,000 years. Research suggests that our original *Homo sapiens* ancestors were likely to have existed in a number of small populations spread out across Africa, some of which migrated out of the continent between 60,000 to 100,000 years ago. Once in Europe and Asia, at some stage in their development, our early Homo sapiens relatives most definitely interacted and interbred with members of the ancient human species Neanderthals and Denisovians. This is shown in the fascinating fact that most modern humans from Europe and Asia carry between two to four percent Neanderthal DNA, whilst those from Melanesia, Papua New Guinea and the indigenous Australian population possess around four to six percent Denisovian DNA. Furthermore, *"everyone with Denisovian ancestry has some amount of Neanderthal ancestry."*[21] This seems to point to the idea that although we are a hybrid mix with links to a rich evolutionary past, in terms of time on the planet we are still relatively new kids on the block.

Additionally, it has been discovered that genetically speaking, as Homo sapiens we are highly related to each other and come from a small base population of approximately 1,000 to 10,000 breeding pairs. This is a possible result of a genetic bottle-neck caused by the Toba mega-volcano eruption on Sumatra, which put the entire globe into what was effectively a ten year plus 'volcanic winter' around 75,000 years ago. The rapid climate change that ensued after this event is thought to have significantly affected human and other wildlife populations. [22]

Therefore, as a species we are much more alike than was originally considered. Whilst similar research into the rest of the Hominid family has shown that all of our great ape cousins, except the bonobo, have much greater genetic diversity amongst members of their species than modern humans.[23] This means that for most of Homo sapiens' time on Earth our populations have remained relatively small until the last 20,000 to 50,000 years.[24] Conversely, for most of ancient history there were far greater numbers of orangutans, gorillas and chimpanzees on the planet than modern humans.[25] However something changed dramatically for us around 50,000 years ago and we began to steadily increase our range and numbers across the globe. [26]

As we stand in the first quarter of the twenty first century, humans number approximately 7.7 billion people with figures rising daily. [27] With an average growth of over 80 million humans added to the global population per annum, we are expected to reach 9 billion by the year 2037.[28] This is estimated to be the human population peak and I will discuss the reasons for this in a later chapter. We are now also positioned as the most populous and widely spread large terrestrial mammal on Earth and can be found living within most latitudes of the planet.

Due to our particular combination of biological and behavioural features we appear able to acclimatize to most environments and adjust to a broad range of terrains. Without a doubt, we are adaptive and resourceful members of the great ape family. Furthermore, if we consider our performance in simplistic biological terms alone with the natural imperative to establish viable populations and pass our genes on to future generations, humanity could be viewed as having been overwhelmingly successful until this point. However, it will be the choices we make today and in the coming years which will determine how successfully we are able to survive into the future.

What are the specific biological characteristics which define us as human and make us distinct from our great ape cousins?

The Human Animal

Over the millennia we have evolved and developed a number of distinctive biological features that have adapted us to life on the planet across a range of diverse environments. These include the following key aspects of our physical make up.

Bipedalism – At some time in history, our human ancestors became bipedal, meaning that we are naturally upright and able to stand, walk and run on two feet. This particular form of locomotion gave us the ability to travel over long distances using a relatively small amount of energy compared to our great ape relatives, as they generally travel on the ground on all four limbs. Whilst, orangutans, which are specifically adapted to arboreal life in the trees, can travel with ease through the forest canopy using all four limbs to swing from tree to tree, grasping with their hands. Interestingly, no animal on the planet can outrun a human over a long period as humans wear out and run down prey over time and distance. We can out-distance any animal on the planet when hunting, and also have a relatively effective ability to run away from those animals which pursue us as their prey. Thus we are extremely adept at running on two feet, particularly over long distances.

Due to our unique form of bipedal, ground-based locomotion, we have evolved a skeleton which is specifically adapted for this purpose. Our hips are narrower and angled in a more bowl shape than other great apes, which allows for the most efficient running gait. Human males have the narrowest hips, enabling them to run faster than human females. Human women's hips are wider to allow for the birth of their offspring, as their babies have large skulls. Unfortunately human females with very narrow hips are more likely to die in child birth. Thus, human women have adapted to have hips that are wider than males' to allow for child birth but that are not too wide to run.

Additionally, we have developed legs that are longer than our arms, with knees and feet aligned to our upright centre of gravity. This is so we can maintain balance whilst standing, walking and running. [29] We do not have opposable toes meaning that we cannot grasp objects with our feet. Our foot bones are more arched than those of other great apes to allow for our bipedalism.[30] As with the other great apes, humans have hands with opposable thumbs. However we have greater movement across our hands with our fingers which gives us excellent fine motor skills and the ability to grasp and hold a variety of objects.

The human shoulder bones are also adapted to facilitate throwing and have a wide scope of movement, which would have assisted with hunting, throwing spears and using some tools and weapons. Conversely, our fellow great apes have shoulders more suited to hanging from trees and quadrupedal ground locomotion. Our skull is shaped to accommodate the well-developed human brain with its enlarged prefrontal cortex and we exhibit flatter facial profiles than other great apes. As an adaptation to our upright stance, our back bone attaches to the middle of the skull and we have a curved lower spine.[31] All these features enable us to effectively perform exceptionally well as bipedal great apes.

Brain Development – Humans display a highly developed brain with a large prefrontal cortex which weighs in at around 1.4 kilograms (three pounds) when fully grown. It was long thought that human brains were the largest as a percentage of body weight in the Animal Kingdom. However, this is incorrect as many birds possess brains which represent up to eight percent of their body weight, whilst the human brain is only approximately 2.5 percent of our total body mass.[32] In relation to other great apes, human brains are around three times the physical size of gorillas and orangutans, yet some regions of these great apes' brains may be just as developed. Although chimpanzees are born with brains of a similar size to those of humans, our brains grow more during our development, especially the prefrontal cortex, making human brains the largest of the great apes. [33] Brain studies have been conducted on members of the great ape family to assess intelligence, but these tests were based upon what is understood about intelligence in humans. However, it is clear that all members of the great ape family display intelligence, understanding, memory and are self-aware, sentient beings.

Tongue and Voice Box – The physical development of the voice box (larynx), tongue and lips in humans has adapted us for speech. This has enabled us to create and verbalise human languages, articulate specific sounds and changes in tone and pitch. [34]These biological features have given us the gift of intricate verbal communication and tonal singing. To facilitate this our voice box is positioned lower down the vocal tract and our necks are longer than in other great apes. The human tongue has greater flexibility and independence, possessing a hyoid muscle that is not attached to any other bones in the body. [35] As previously mentioned, humans also display a flatter facial profile and our mouths and canine teeth are different from those of other great apes. These biological characteristics mean that humans have developed the unique ability to communicate via speech, which would have contributed to our survival as a species.

Hair – Humans display thick and prolific hair growth on specific parts of their bodies, such as their head, under arms and genital areas. In maturity, males can also have facial hair. Other great apes possess hair covering most regions of their body. Humans also have hair follicles and hair over most parts of their skin, however this bodily hair is fine, short and lighter than that of our great ape relatives. [36] As such, although we appear to be somewhat naked or hairless apes this is actually an incorrect observation. It is thought that, as a cooling mechanism our ability to sweat and hence reduce our bodily heat, is assisted by our lack of dense hair covering. It has also been discovered that our superior sweat glands enhance our ability to maintain body temperatures during long distance running. Species that rely on panting as a cooling strategy can over-heat whilst attempting the long distance travel achievable by humans.

Reproduction – Human reproduction also demonstrates some interesting variations from that of other great apes, which may have increased our survival as a species. These variations include the fact that human females have developed a process of menopause, which means that they are unable to reproduce in later life. We are the only great ape to possess this adaptation. Humans have therefore been able to take advantage of the older non-child bearing females in their families and tribes, to help raise the following generations of young. Grandmothers help to improve the survival of their children's children, thereby increasing their own genetic success and, in many ways, the overall survival of the tribe.[37] They offer additional support and care for children and mothers during the intensive early years of child raising. Grandmothers also held key roles within the tribe as matriarchs and the cultural stores of wisdom and knowledge, as well as being healers and herbalists who could assist the tribe with health challenges and injuries. Grandmothers therefore were a valuable addition to tribal life and a useful adaptive strategy for humans.

For most primate females, reproduction and the raising of offspring is 'expensive' in terms of the demands upon her body, time and resources whilst these aspects are comparatively 'cheap' for males. The differences in levels of investment in human children, together with the inherent dangers of reproduction, increases the need for human females to be capable of being highly selective in their choice of mate.

Interestingly, under certain circumstances, human females also appear to display instances where the natural love bond between mother and baby is not 'switched-on' at birth. This sometimes occurs if a human mother gives birth under socially, emotionally or physically stressful circumstances. If so, she may not produce the deep love bonding hormones at birth which enable her to form the all-important connection with her child. This type of disconnection between mother and baby is somewhat different from that of female gorillas, who can abandon a once loved child after a new dominant male takes over her harem. The female gorilla does this in order to ensure protection by the male, because in gorilla groups the dominant male prioritizes protection of those females raising his offspring. In the case of human females, if this lack of bond with her infant is caused by a biological imperative similar to that of gorillas, this may serve as a survival mechanism for the mother. This is because the mother can go on to reproduce later when her circumstances improve, whilst the baby will most likely perish releasing the mother from the current stress under which she is placed. Therefore, when mothers do not bond with their babies, it may be a biologically driven situation and one that has evolved and adapted us for biological success. NB: Although there can be a myriad of causative factors in cases such as these for human mothers, here I am specially addressing the biological drivers involved.

Another biological adaptation that has helped to make humans more successful as a species is the existence of homosexual men. As it has been discovered that epigenetics, a process by which specific genes can be switched on, in this case in-utero, are activated to 'switch on' the homosexual gene in some male babies. Research has found that a mother's likelihood of giving birth to a gay son depends upon on how many previous sons she has had, as well as whether she was sick during her pregnancy. [38] In both cases, the gay gene can be activated and switched-on in the womb because the mother will need more nurturing support and assistance to care for the family. Rather than another typically boisterous hetero-sexual son, a gay son will be more able and likely to provide the strong, connected support she will require to raise the family. Thus, her gay son will help to increase the survival of the family and her genes. [39]

Homosexual men have also helped the survival of the tribe

by reducing the competition for a female mate. They often became shamans, cultural icons and socially intelligent advisors as well as excellent fighters who would go off and defend the tribe. Free from attachments to the women and children, gay men made excellent soldiers who would often fight alongside their lovers to protect their tribe.

Male Aggression – Human male aggression appears to be an adaptation for survival of our species connected to our hunter-gatherer past.[40] Accordingly, male humans display an ability to switch-on their aggressive and violent characteristics, whilst switching-off their compassion in times of war and defence of the tribe. Men will gather in fighting parties, much like common chimpanzees, and in these groups are capable of committing atrocities and war crimes in the name of defending the tribe. At the same time they will form strong bonds of mateship and camaraderie with their fellow warriors and will often perform great feats of bravery to protect their mates.[41]

Furthermore, if one of their own is killed or even threatened by the enemy, human males are capable of retribution and violence towards their foe. It appears that with the switch-off mechanism, males can also actually enjoy the experience of conflict and gain satisfaction from it. Interestingly, this element of the process can cause great stress for modern day soldiers once they return to normal life. This may occur when they cannot come to terms with what they have seen, what they have done and the fact that at some point they may have enjoyed some aspects of the process. Post-traumatic stress can result from this, even though their behaviour can be explained as an evolutionary adaptation for survival. Such aggressive male behaviour and violence towards those perceived as enemies may well have given us a greater chance of survival in the past.[42]

The specific physical characteristics and evolutionary behaviours which distinguish humans from other members of the great ape family are also the same traits that have made us well adapted to life on Earth. However, our close relatives, the great apes, were also able to thrive and evolve over millions of years, with each being uniquely adapted to their specific habitats. Whilst we as humans undoubtedly display biological differences from our great ape cousins, modern science has revealed that we are more closely related and similar than we ever dreamed. Most importantly, perhaps it is when we begin to focus upon the similarities between us and our great ape cousins that we can begin to see ourselves and them in a different light.

As I shared in my last book, 'Orangutans My Cousins, My Friends,' my first opportunity to meet and interact with orangutans was as a trained biologist and professional zookeeper. Therefore it was through these eyes that I initially viewed them, however it wouldn't be long before I came to see them from a quite different perspective.

Seeing Through the Eyes of a Biologist

My journey to explore and expand my understanding of humanity began in earnest when, as a fresh faced Biology Graduate, I landed my dream job at Perth Zoo in September 1986. It would only be a matter of time before I became part of the Primate Section of the zoo and came into direct contact with our great ape cousins, the enigmatic orangutans as well as the lively and expressive chimpanzees. However, I must say that it was the more thoughtful and inquisitive orangutans which most intrigued me. So as you can imagine I was keen to interact with these fascinating beings as much as I could.

When that day finally came, I was shown how to clean their enclosures, given their diet sheets and instructed on how and when to feed them. From there, I was pretty much left to get on with it. For me this was an exciting and life changing opportunity. To begin with, because of what I knew about the orangutans' relatively non-confrontational behaviour, I didn't worry too much that they were physically stronger than me. Nor was I too concerned that they could be potentially dangerous when under stress. As I knew that selected members of the Primate Team used to go in to the enclosures with some of the orangutans in the past. Therefore, in my mind I had a clear slate so to speak and I thought, "Oh well, I'll go in with them and see what happens," and that is just what I did.

Therefore, I began to go into the enclosures and sit with the orangutans whilst I had my lunch. This was definitely not usual practice in any other zoos to my knowledge. Mainly I chose to interact with the female orangutans such as Utama, Puteri, Punya and Puspa or with the younger adolescent males such as Puluh. I felt no fear when I was with them, just a calm sense of awe and appreciation. In fact, I saw it as an enormous privilege to spend this time with the orangutans at such close quarters. I would observe their particular behaviours and attitudes towards me as each orangutan had their own very distinct personalities. Yet all were highly intelligent, aware beings. Over time, I came to really like them as 'persons' and felt an affinity and innate connection with them. What was even more rewarding was they appeared to like, and wished to connect with me too. So for both myself and the orangutans it was a case of the more we got to know each other, the more we grew to like each other.

We Are Great Apes

> 'We admit that we are like apes, but we
> seldom realise that we are apes.'
> Richard Dawkins

With the completion of the genome sequencing of all members of the great ape family, we now recognise that as living beings we are all directly related. This is evidenced by the following percentages of genetic match between us and other great apes:

- Chimpanzees and bonobos share approximately 99 percent of human DNA,
- Gorillas share approximately 98 percent of human DNA, and
- Orangutans share approximately 97 percent of human DNA.

As life forms we are more similar than different and more closely related than not. In fact, these landmark results prove that we each possessed a common African based ancestor at some point in our evolutionary past. Instead of humans evolving from our great ape cousins in a linear progression and direct family tree, our relatedness is represented more accurately by a branched cluster in which each great ape species has a shared ancestor. At some point in the distant past, great ape family members diverged and followed their own unique evolutionary path. According to research, we last shared a common ancestor with chimpanzees and bonobos, our closest genetic relatives, around five to six million years ago. Whilst, it is considered that gorillas diverged from a common ancestor around eight to ten million years ago, and orangutans approximately twelve to sixteen million years ago. [43] From these points of divergence, each member of the great ape family went on to develop into a distinct species over millions of years of evolution. Through the process of natural selection and the development of rich cultural knowledge all species have become highly evolved and suited to their own natural habitats.

Interestingly, orangutans and humans are the only remaining great apes to have successfully migrated out of Africa. Orangutans are known to have existed in China and India before finding their way into South East Asia and to their current Bornean and Sumatran homes. Whilst the members of the chimpanzee, bonobo and gorilla species are still only found in the wild in Africa. However, although we diverged along our evolutionary paths as a family we each share common physical features and a range of biologically driven behaviours.

What are the specific biological characteristics which we share with all great apes as distinct from other primates?

Body and Brain Size

The great apes are named as such due to their appreciably larger body size as compared to other primates and lesser apes. For example, gorillas can reach a size of anywhere between 1.4 to 1.8 metres (4.5 to 6 feet) in height when standing, and weigh as much as 200 kilograms (440 pounds) or more. Mature adult male orangutans can grow to a height of around 1.5 metres (5 feet) tall and weigh up to 140 kilograms (264 to 309 pounds) with an arm span of up to 2.4metres (8 feet) wide. Chimpanzees and bonobos are smaller than other great apes, but are still physically strong and agile. Humans display the greatest variety in size and weight across the great ape family.

All great apes have larger and more complex brains compared to other primates allowing for greater intelligence, memory and learning abilities, and making each member an aware, sentient being. As mentioned earlier, humans have the largest brain however it has been suggested that, of the other great apes, orangutans have the most similar brain development to humans.

Large Skull and Molar Development

To accommodate our more developed brains, great apes possess larger skulls than other primates and this comes with a commonality within the lower jaw bone and teeth. All great apes have a set of distinctive molar teeth to assist them with chewing and digesting their predominantly plant based diets. In terms of diet, orangutans, gorillas and bonobos are mainly vegetarian with some supplementation of termites, ants, insects and perhaps the occasional consumption of meat. Whilst chimpanzees and humans appear to be more omnivorous by choice and eat meat as part of their diet to a greater or lesser degree.

Shoulder Structure

The specific structure of great apes' shoulders and arms allow for improved movement and rotation. As a result great apes are able to swing beneath branches of trees if travelling above the ground. This is best displayed amongst orangutans, which spend the majority of their lives in their arboreal habitat. The distinctive great ape shoulder and arm structure also enables climbing and tool use and is complimented by hands which have an opposable thumb. This provides greater dexterity and the ability to carry objects and food. Great apes also have a skeletal structure which features a wide ribcage to form a relatively shallow chest cavity. [44]

Offspring

All great apes invest much time and effort into rearing and caring for their young, with the female orangutan known to be the most maternally nurturing mothers of all living beings, even more so than human mothers. This is because great apes each possess cultural knowledge and distinctive social structures that must be passed down to their young. Thus they learn to interact and survive via culture. As mentioned earlier, great apes also demonstrate similar gestation periods and tend to give birth to single offspring.

Blood Types

Great apes share the same blood groups, with the common types of A, B, AB and O present in each species. It is thought that these common blood groups developed over 20 million years ago. [45]

This also contributes to the fact that great apes can share and spread diseases such as hepatitis, measles, polio, scabies and other communicable illnesses across species.

Upon considering the specific biological features and commonalities shared by all great apes it is clear why we classify ourselves as members of the same family as these remarkable beings. Not only do we share common ancestry with our great ape cousins, we are also incredibly similar biologically. Unfortunately, the latest figures from the IUCN Red List show that seven out of eight species of great apes are currently threatened with extinction. With both the bonobos and chimpanzees on the Endangered Species list and each species of orangutans and gorillas listed as Critically Endangered and all wild populations are under threat. [46] Tellingly, humans are the only great ape missing from the list with our populations continuing to expand at a rapid rate.

Why is this so?

In part, it comes down to how we see ourselves. On one hand we understand that we are great apes, however, at the same time we also perceive ourselves as separate and different from our great ape cousins. We thus treat them accordingly, as though they are of lesser importance and value than we are. As humans we are able to stand by as their habitats are destroyed, they are needlessly slaughtered and their species are pushed to the brink of extinction. We do this even though we understand it doesn't have to be this way. On a broader level we know that we are a part of the Animal Kingdom, yet we often do not consider ourselves animals. This is a contradiction in itself, as we are biological animals. As such, there exists within us an ability to see some facts clearly, but ignore or remain consciously blind to others. However, at some level our unconscious and often contradictory ways of perceiving are impacting our thinking and our actions on the planet. Unfortunately, the cost is being born by our great ape cousins, who are unable to protect themselves from the consequences of these, as their shrinking numbers so clearly indicate.

For me the following experiment illustrates some of our conditioned ways of seeing.

Ways of Seeing

In 1999 a pair of research psychologists at Harvard University, Christopher Chabris and Dan Simons, created a video titled 'Gorilla in Our Midst.'[47] The video was part of a group experiment involving their students and was designed to study how humans see and recall events when asked to focus their attention on one particular activity. At the time Chabris was a lecturer and research associate and Simons was his teaching assistant at the Harvard Psychology Department.[48] The resulting visual experiment, now commonly referred to as 'The Invisible Gorilla,' has proved to be one of the most surprisingly effective pieces of research into human selective attention and how we *see*.

Here's how the experiment runs. At the beginning of *The Invisible Gorilla* video, viewers are informed that they are to participate in a short selective attention test. It is explained that in the video, there will be two teams of people throwing basketballs to each other, one wearing white T-shirts and the other wearing black T-shirts. Viewers are instructed to count the number of times the members of the white T-shirt team pass the basketball to each other during the video. At the end of the exercise, each participant is asked for their scores. Once they have been given this one task and a single focus, the video is played for them. However, what participants report after watching the video is astonishing.

This is because, in the middle of the video a student dressed as a big hairy black gorilla walks into the midst of the teams from the right hand side of the picture, whilst the teams continue to throw the balls around and make passes. The gorilla stops and stands in the centre of the frame, thumps its chest like Tarzan and then casually walks off to the left of the picture. All up, the gorilla is in the video for a full nine seconds. Startlingly, when participants are asked what they saw whilst watching the video, routinely around 50 percent of the group miss the gorilla entirely.

Even more interestingly, these participants state with total honesty that there was no gorilla in the video - they literally did not see it. Half of the audience, who understand that they are participating in a selective attention test, do not register the presence of the gorilla during the video. These statistics seem to hold true with different audiences over time, and count numbers for the basketball passes also vary in accuracy. [49] Once the results are in and the video is replayed, of course, the whole audience can see the gorilla and everyone is amazed that they missed it to begin with. What is happening here? How are intelligent, fully sighted, capable humans not able to see something as obvious as a gorilla standing right before their eyes?

Seeing What We Focus Upon

It all comes down to how human beings see. The beauty and the efficacy of this visual test brings to light a couple of important facts about how we as humans perceive the world around us and our place within it. Neuroscience has shown that whilst humans physiologically look with our eyes we see and make sense of what's happening around us with our brain. [50] Much like a camera used by an experienced photographer, our eyes act as the mechanical device to collect visual data under the specific direction of the operator, or in our case, our brain. Understanding that a photographer selects what will be photographed and can also use a variety of techniques and processes to create the desired picture.

In the same way our brain can determine what visual information our eyes will seek and how we will view it. This means, the sensory information which the human eye conveys to the brain is heavily influenced by those things to which our brain directs us to pay attention. Conversely, responding to instruction from the brain, our eyes can filter out information which is deemed as superfluous, unimportant or un-necessary. Thus, what we think we are experiencing as reality is a combination of filtered visual information provided by our eyes, which is then processed and seen according to our brains' internal biases and perspectives. Therefore what we see as real is very much determined by what our mind prioritises and directs us to focus upon.

This aspect of seeing what we focus upon in the external world is clearly demonstrated by *The Invisible Gorilla* experiment. The participants who did not see the gorilla were so busy focusing upon the task of counting basketball passes amongst the white team, they screened out the visual information of the gorilla passing across the screen. Experiencing what Professor Simons calls in-attentional blindness, students were unable to see an obvious element of the video because of the effectiveness of their internal filtering mechanisms. This demonstrates that when humans focus on pre-determined specifics or actively seek to find information aligned with a certain intention we can become selective in what we see. Importantly, we don't even realise that we are doing so.

Even though we know that around 50 percent of viewers did see the gorilla, there were also discrepancies in the number of white team passes counted among both the group that noticed the gorilla and the group that did not. Therefore, viewers also saw things differently in this regard too. This brings into question how accurately we see and experience external events and recall details. Ultimately, what this simple video and its results show is that humans don't actually see everything which occurs around them. We are capable of making mistakes as well as actively ignoring or missing information which does not align with our world view.[51] As a result we often see what we focus on and we have blind spots in areas that may not be deemed important within our perception.

This finding alone certainly raises questions about our understanding of how we perceive reality, because when we focus upon the differences instead of the similarities between ourselves and our fellow living beings that is what we see. On the other hand, when we seek to find the common ground we share, it is easy for us to see and appreciate. This is one of the shifts we need to make in how we view ourselves and other living beings. We must come to view them as intelligent, aware sentient life forms who are worthy of protection and care so that they can live wild and free in their natural environments.

This was definitely how I began to see our orangutan cousins as I saw their innate humanity.

Meeting Pulang

During my time within the Primate Section I had the privilege of forming deep bonds of friendship with most of the orangutans within our care. This meant that I was also able to be closely involved with around six to seven successful orangutan births as part of our breeding program. In this way I was given the opportunity to become part of their unique world which was something that not many other people have had the privilege of witnessing.

One of these experiences was with Puan, a 40 year old female orangutan, and the birth of her very active and cheeky baby, Pulang. However, Puan was not the happiest nor the most trusting of orangutans. This was due to her past experiences as a young, wild-born orangutan who had witnessed the slaughter of her mother and had then been held in Johor Zoo, Malaysia. Therefore, as the birth of this baby approached she was quite secretive in her behaviours, which meant that it was difficult for us to accurately judge when the event would occur.

In the meantime, I began staying overnight in close proximity to the orangutan night quarters so I could be on call for Puan's impending labour. I had also arranged for a small film crew to record the birth. However, each time we would set up for filming, expecting the birth to occur, Puan did not go into labour. In this way, as we waited for her baby to arrive, days turned into weeks and I became a regular night-time feature in the area around the orangutan night quarters as I continued to sleep there awaiting the birth.

Finally, Puan began to show clear signs of the impending labour and we were rewarded with the arrival of a beautiful little female named Pulang. Her name literally meaning 'to go home' in Indonesian, as I was now able to return home to my bed after all this time of sleeping at the zoo. Luckily we were also able to film this special event as the first recorded live orangutan birth. Since this time Pulang's birth has been watched online by over 2,000,000 viewers.

As always I must say that it was definitely love at first sight when I laid eyes on little Pulang. Because there is another interesting difference between orangutan and human babies, and this is that orangutan young seem to be born aware and awake. They also seem able to see very quickly and to interact with their mothers and the environment. In fact, very soon after they are born you can appreciate their unique and vibrant little personalities within their eyes

In addition to this, there were two other very special events which occurred after the birth of every baby orangutan with which I was involved. Events which would fill my heart with awe and gratitude and also cement my deep love and connection with these beings. The same was true of Puan and Pulang. Firstly within 48 hours of giving birth the orangutan mothers would bring their babies as close as possible to me. From there they would offer their baby's outstretched hand towards me so the baby could grasp my fingers within theirs as a way of bonding.

Secondly, often shortly after this the mothers would also give me their baby to hold by gently and deliberately placing their infant into my arms.

It is events like these which I treasured for their beauty, truth and impact upon my life. Additionally, I was beginning to make big changes within as I was no longer able to view orangutans, or any of the great apes, as being different from me. In fact, I had come to the conclusion that they were not only sentient beings but persons in the true sense of the word. Therefore, it would be my interactions with these remarkable beings which would cause me to question exactly where the boundaries of humanity began and ended. This was because when I looked into the eyes of the orangutans, I could see humanity looking back at me. Interestingly, I was to later find that I wasn't alone in my experience.

Chapter Two
Human Nature and the
Chimpanzee Mind

'We are enslaved by anything we do not consciously see.
We are freed by conscious perception.'
Vernon Howard

Human Nature

For most of us, the name Charles Darwin (1809–1882) is synonymous with the theory of evolution and natural selection. A British naturalist and biologist, Darwin is widely recognised for his ground-breaking book, "*On the Origin of Species,*" in which he explains his theories in detail.[52] Attributed with discovering and unlocking the secrets behind these powerful biological mechanisms, Darwin and his works forever changed the way we view ourselves as part of the living world. However, it is a lesser known fact that Darwin did not develop his theories in isolation or that he collaborated with fellow British naturalist, explorer and anthropologist, Alfred Russel Wallace (1823–1913). Together, Darwin and Wallace wrote and published a paper in 1858 outlining their concepts of evolution and natural selection, a year before the publication of Darwin's seminal book. [53] Thus, in many ways they were not only respected contemporaries but co-creators of this foundational biological theory.

Intriguingly, as part of their research into evolution, both Darwin and Wallace shared a common interest in the fellow members of the great ape family, specifically orangutans. This was because each of these intellectual greats were able to closely observe and interact with live orangutans whilst developing their theories. [54] Yet even though their respective experiences and the conditions under which they conducted their investigations were worlds apart, they both made similar observations about the strikingly human-like nature and behaviours of our orange cousins. In that they could each perceive the humanity which the orangutans displayed. This humanity was something of which I was becoming increasingly aware of the longer I worked with our orange cousins at the zoo.

Firstly, Darwin was able to interact and study a couple of captive orangutans named Jenny and Tommy at London's Zoological Gardens in 1838. During his visits Darwin was struck by what he saw as not only behavioural similarities but also commonalities between humans and orangutans in their innate nature. Amongst the observations he made were that Jenny displayed a relatively calm temperament unless she was teased or 'vexed' by her keepers. Darwin was present one day when a keeper showed Jenny an apple and then refused to give it to her. Here Darwin witnessed the young orangutan become increasingly upset and annoyed, showing her displeasure by crying and throwing herself on the ground in a tantrum, much like a human child. However, once the keeper spoke to Jenny and reassured her that she could have the apple if she calmed down, Jenny was able to do so and was rewarded with the apple. Upon receiving the fruit, she immediately sat on a chair and happily ate it as a human child would. [55]

Darwin also noted that Jenny was fond of playing with sticks, straw and other objects made available to her in her cage. She would either arrange the straw in lines or use the sticks as tools. For example, she used the sticks as potential levers by inserting them into holes or as deterrents to keep other animals or humans at bay. Jenny also liked soft objects and decided to place a couple of handkerchiefs on her head as an apparent imitation of the hats that her human visitors tended to wear. However, it is now known that wild orangutans often place leaves on their heads to protect themselves from sun or rain.

When calm, Jenny was curious, inquisitive and playful. She was also able to follow instructions given to her by the keepers. In fact, Darwin felt that she seemed able to understand some of the English language.[56] However, it was perhaps both Jenny's and Tommy's response to a mirror that Darwin had placed into the cage that allowed him to see the level of self-awareness displayed by these young orangutans. Both of the orangutans closely examined the mirror, looking into the glass, touching its surface, moving around and striking poses in front of it, looking behind the mirror and even ignoring it. Darwin noted that, after some time, he felt that Jenny was happy to observe and groom herself in front of the mirror. This meant that she knew that she was seeing herself in the reflection, demonstrating she was self-aware as a separate being. [57]

Ultimately, the research visits Darwin conducted with these orangutans confirmed his belief that orangutans and other great apes were our relatives and that we shared a common ancestor. His observations convinced him that human emotions and behavioural patterns were also present in great apes. Perhaps most importantly, he famously stated that, *"The difference between humans and animals was of degree, not of kind."* [58]

In contrast, Wallace's interactions with both live and dead orangutans occurred in 1855, during his 17-month stay in Sarawak, Borneo. A man of his time, he was conducting a hunting and collecting expedition to the area as part of his research and development of his theories. It was on this expedition that he killed and collected a wide range of wild animals, including orangutans. All up it is recorded that he shot and killed at least 17 orangutans of differing size, gender and age. Each of these he treated as specimens, which meant that he meticulously measured, skinned and dissected these orangutans and sent their preserved skins and skeletons back to Britain. For these he received payment, so they were considered highly valuable artefacts from his trip as well as a way of funding his expedition. However, even though he was comfortable with personally slaughtering such a large number of orangutans, he did mention in a note on some of Darwin's work, that he considered orangutans to share a common ancestor with humans. [59]

In 1869 Wallace published a detailed account of his many close encounters with orangutans in his book, "*The Malay Archipelago.*" [60] Whilst the descriptions of his hunting exploits seem both cold-hearted and unthinkable in modern terms, he did ascribe a number of human-like characteristics to the orangutans he encountered. These are included in vivid explanations of how he executed his hunts. For example, in one section he recounts finding a sub-adult male feeding in a tree, whereby Wallace shot the orangutan and it immediately fell from the tree. As the orangutan appeared to be relatively unharmed, the male quickly made his way to the closest tree and started to climb up its trunk to escape. Wallace fired some more bullets into the orangutan and it fell once more, this time with a broken arm and wounds to its body. At this point, two of Wallace's Dayak assistants ran to the dying being and, each taking one hand of the orangutan, attempted to secure his arms to a pole. However, even in his injured state the male was too strong for the men and they had to let him go in fear that he may have bitten them. Bloody and wounded, the orangutan made one last attempt to escape back to safety and began slowly climbing another tree. At this point, Wallace declared that to, "*...avoid trouble, I shot it through the heart.*" [61]

Shocking and brutal as Wallace's accounts are, he mentions many of the male orangutans he killed grabbing at their wounds as a person would, moaning in pain and also displaying anger and even indignation at being shot. However, at no time did these beings, which are up to seven times stronger than human males, attack Wallace or his men unless under threat or cornered when injured. In these instances the orangutans would bite their attackers only to escape from harm.

Furthermore when Wallace described his encounters with female orangutans, especially those with babies, he mentions that in all cases the females would break off branches and fruit to throw at him and his assistants as a way of warding them off. He makes the observation that those females with babies were exercising their strong parental instincts to protect their young. In one case, he recounts how he shot down a large female orangutan from a tree, to discover that she had a baby, which had been flung into a muddy bank of the nearby river during the fall. The baby was still alive, so Wallace decided to take the orphaned infant home with him to keep as a pet.

Over the first few weeks he remarks how expressive and child like the young orangutan was and referred to the being as his 'sweet baby.' He even captured a small monkey to keep the baby orangutan company and observed how human-like the orangutan infant was in comparison to the highly active monkey. Unfortunately, after approximately three months, the youngster fell ill with fever and died. At this point, Wallace expressed his sadness and sense of loss at losing his entertaining and amusing companion. Shortly afterwards he skinned the baby, preserving its skin and skeleton for delivery back to England, where his agent would handle their sale.

From these examples of how both Darwin and Wallace viewed the innate human-ness of the orangutans they each closely observed, the question begs to be asked, *"How could intelligent, educated individuals, who recognised the innate biological and behavioural similarities between orangutans and humans, fail to see that to treat them as lesser beings was unacceptable?"* It comes down to a phenomenon known in psychology as cognitive dissonance.

Cognitive Dissonance

Cognitive dissonance is a way of seeing that allows us to hold contradictory or conflicting ideas, beliefs, attitudes, perceptions and ideologies at the same time. This state often causes inner discomfort as old ways of seeing or understanding the world are brought into question by the arrival of new information, facts or experiences. These new perspectives can result in us challenging our existing ideas or values. However, when we still choose to hold onto the old ways of seeing we can experience another effect of cognitive dissonance. As we become blind to any information that makes us question our established attitudes and can even reject it based upon the internal blind spot we have in our beliefs. Therefore, even though cognitive dissonance is experienced where we encounter inconsistency within our thoughts, we can either choose to alter our perspective or elect to ignore the new data altogether.

In the case of Wallace, he was recognised as an intellectual great of his time and was deeply interested in the natural world. As a man of moral and academic standing, his theories were ground-breaking and caused much outcry when first released, yet he stood by his convictions. He saw humanity in the orangutans he killed, but as a person of his time his cognitive dissonance did not allow him to see the orangutans as sentient persons. This is because the strengths of his cultural beliefs and ways of seeing were too strong to enable this recognition. Similarly, even today many humans are still unwilling or unable to recognise this truth.

However, it is possible to break through the restrictive limits of cognitive dissonance by firstly bringing its existence to our awareness. From this point we can become more conscious of our ways of seeing and begin to identify where we may be experiencing conflicting beliefs and contradictory behaviours. As a consequence, we can begin to develop greater discernment in our perceptions of new facts and information by educating ourselves on an ongoing basis. This means we are always learning and keeping our minds and hearts open to alternative views. For example, I would experience my own form of cognitive dissonance whilst I worked in a zoo and cared for the captive orangutans there. This was because I was also an animal lover who believed that living beings were best left in their wild, free, state wherever possible. An incident early in my career helped me begin to see the inner contradictions within and put me on a path towards shifting my perspective.

Seeing the Cracks Appear

In my early days as a zookeeper I arranged a working holiday to the United States of America (USA). Whilst there I was able to visit a number of zoos around the country as a way of increasing my professional understanding in the field. It was an eye-opening experience and I was able to gain an inside view of many established zoos within the USA. I had also long heard of a well-known oceanarium which featured dolphins, orcas (killer whales), seals and other marine animals as part of its captive collection. Thinking that it would be amazing to visit the facility and see one of their famous live shows with the marine mammals as the stars, I purchased a ticket for a day pass. I'm embarrassed to admit it, but at the time, I was particularly looking forward to seeing the dolphins and orcas performing live and interacting with their trainers and the audience.

Sitting down to watch the first show, I felt anticipation at the opportunity to be so close to these intelligent, graceful beings and to be a part of the spectacle about to commence. However, once it began, I started to feel a sense of unease at what I was witnessing. The slick, visually entertaining performance showcased massive orcas, agile dolphins and playful seals doing synchronised tricks, acrobatic feats and aquatic dance routines under the careful supervision of their handlers. Orchestrated with split second precision, these remarkable marine mammals were directed to perform their parts in the show to the audience's delight. In fact, from the crowd's responses, everyone seemed to be enjoying the show, but for me something felt not quite right. As my discomfort grew, I watched on, somehow present but also strangely distanced from what was happening in front of me. It felt as if I was glimpsing the truth of what this performance meant for the beings who were forced to participate. What I was seeing wasn't good.

I was relieved when the performance finally finished. Everyone in the audience around me was cheering, clapping and calling out in appreciation and applause. However, I didn't clap. Instead, I sat there in a state of shock, caught momentarily in a world of my own in which time slowed down for a few seconds. Aware that something was deeply wrong with what I had just been a part of but unsure of exactly what, I couldn't shake-off my lingering feeling of disquiet. I left and returned to my accommodation with a range of unexpected thoughts and feelings turning over in my mind.

This was an unsettling event because I was experiencing cognitive dissonance at the point at which my beliefs and ways of seeing the world were brushing up against a different, more compassionate version of reality. I had recognised during the show that it was neither right nor fair that these intelligent, marine mammals be taken from the wild, held captive and forced to perform for a viewing public. However, I couldn't put my finger on why it had affected me so much because as a zookeeper, I too was a part of a system that kept intelligent self-aware, beings imprisoned against their will. As such, it could be said that I was part of the same structure. Yet, I loved animals and felt that I was doing the best I could to make their lives better within the zoo environment. So my inability to see the contradictory nature of my beliefs and behaviours was clouding the inner recognition of a greater truth. The truth was that keeping sentient living beings captive is in no way beneficial for the *animals, in fact it is inhumane and cruel.*

Ultimately, most people now understand that the capture, captivity and training of marine mammals, such as killer whales, for entertainment at venues like this is a horrific experience for these beings. They are often kept isolated, away from others of their kind, in tiny holding tanks where they are unable to swim and move freely. This treatment is abusive on many levels for these social beings, as they are wild creatures adapted to living in family pods in the world's vast oceans. In circumstances such as the oceanarium, they have been stolen from their marine homes and no longer have decision-making power or choice in their lives. However, before this cruelty was brought to the attention of the general public in a number of documentaries and media reports, many of us innocently went along with their existence. Neither did we recognise the incongruence or the truth of the situation straight away. This is how cognitive dissonance operates within the human mind and it can prevent us from seeing the facts that are right in front of us. This was the case for me when I visited this oceanarium, and during my early days at the zoo.

However the cracks were beginning to form in how I saw zoos and the rights of the captive self-aware beings held within their walls. I just couldn't quite see through those cracks to the other side at that time. But they would only continue to widen as my awareness developed. This was because I was beginning to understand that orangutans and other sentient living beings such as great apes, orcas and elephants were actually persons in their own right and possessed awareness, intelligence, memory, culture, communication and language systems of their own. Indeed, once you can perceive them as persons you don't have to explain why they deserve to be treated with compassion and live wild and free. As this becomes self-evident.

How do we begin to see our great ape cousins as persons?

Seeing the Ape in Us and the Humanity in the Ape

In addition to the many biological similarities we share with our great ape cousins, we also display a similar range of behavioural and socially based traits. Unsurprisingly, when we look to find the similarities and commonalities between us, it is here that we discover just how closely aligned we are.

Culture

It is often said that our culture is what sets humans apart from the other great apes. However, all members of the great ape family demonstrate rich and diverse culture. This is because great apes adapt to their environment via culture and learned behaviours. In doing so, they provide their young and their social groups with the best opportunity to survive and thrive into the future. Orangutans, chimpanzees and gorillas each display learned customs and traditions, which are passed down from generation to generation and across their social structures. Furthermore, as these customs and traditions can be linked to specific habitats, specific groups have their own unique and highly developed forms of culture. These can differ from region to region and group to group.

The reason that the transfer of culture within great ape societies is so critical for their survival is linked to their relatively low levels of instinctive behaviours compared with other living beings. For example, the cubs of a high-order predator such as a tiger are born with approximately 90 percent instinct and acquire 10 percent learned culture. For tigers there are generally many offspring born to one female. Thus, as a being which relies on refined instinctive behaviours to survive, there is less maternal rearing and transmission of culture to the cubs. In this way, tigers are more subject to the forces of natural selection. However, great apes are born with approximately 10 percent instinct and a corresponding need for 90 percent learned culture. This, combined with low offspring numbers, (with one highly dependent infant generally born at a time) means that the period of maternal care and parenting for all great ape young is long in comparison. It is during this extended period of child rearing that culture is passed down to the young, helping them to adapt to their environment. Therefore, because they adapt via culture, great apes are necessarily highly intelligent.

For great apes this is a successful strategy and allows them to respond to environmental change much faster than would natural selection alone. However this only works well if there are no predators, because if even relatively small proportions of females are lost, the species can become endangered. This is occurring for the other great apes due to human predation and large scale destruction of their habitats. Unfortunately, this is one of the key reasons that all other members of the great ape family are threatened with extinction. As such, the strategy of adapting via culture, which has helped them to evolve and survive as intelligent, sentient beings, is also a mechanism by which their existence is endangered.

Examples of cultural learning within orangutans are many and can be observed in their vast knowledge of edible foods and their spatial and seasonal locations within the forest. Orangutans also build specialised nests high in the tree top canopy each night as a place to sleep as well as a way of protecting themselves from predators. Each nest is constructed in a specific way using the trees found in their habitats and are formed using an intricate criss-crossed pattern of interwoven tree branches, leaves and twigs. When they know that it will rain orangutans also build protective leaf roofs for their nests. For extra comfort they will make themselves a soft cushion of leaves and small branches. Latest research also shows that orangutans have their own form of medicine and will use locally sourced plants and herbs to help themselves recover from diseases such as malaria. Amazingly, when researchers checked with the local indigenous people of the area as to which forest plants they used for the same illnesses, they confirmed that they also used these plants and herbs.

Another form of cultural learning is tool use. All great apes use tools for various reasons such as sourcing food and water, creating shelter, defending themselves, testing distance and water depth, grooming and play. Within populations of wild orangutans the use of 42 different tools has been recorded. [62]

Fu Manchu the Escaping Orangutan

My exposure to the orangutans in captivity within zoos demonstrated to me their ingenious powers of observation, imitation, tool use and creative problem solving ability. As they are, without a doubt, master escape artists. In my last book, I shared many of the orangutan's successful escape plans that I had witnessed first-hand. Yet perhaps one of the most famous escapees was a male orangutan named Fu Manchu who was a resident at Omaha Zoo in the USA. A serial escape artist, Fu was able to leave his enclosure at the zoo during one spree of four consecutive escapes. He did this by walking down into a dry moat in his enclosure and, from there he climbed down some air vents to gain access to a locked maintenance door. At this point he was observed by his keepers to take a piece of wire shaped as a lock pick from his mouth and use this to open the door. Once the door was open, it was out into the freedom of the zoo grounds for Fu Manchu.[63]

Not only had Fu been hiding his hand made key in his mouth to facilitate his escapes when the opportunity arose, but during one of his adventures he managed to take a companion and three baby orangutans with him. As I often say, if a zookeeper tells you that they have never had an orangutan escape, they are either not telling the truth or simply haven't worked with orangutans long enough.

Social

All great apes, except the orangutans are highly social beings living in structured groups of differing sizes. Highly interactive, chimpanzees can form large social communities up to 100 strong, which are often governed by a coalition of males. Bonobos are highly social and are recognised for their matriarchal social structure as well their use of sexual behaviours to bond, greet each other, offer comfort and interact. Gorillas form smaller family groups around a dominant male with a harem of unrelated females and their babies.

Orangutans are semi solitary great apes who live in territories spread out across the forest. The males are the gender that disperses and they will set up a territory in the rainforest, using their long calls to attract fertile females to their nest to mate. Often, once they have mated with all the females in the area, males will move off to seek new territories and mature females. On the other hand the females will set up a territory close to her mother's so you will find that all the females in a given areas are related with overlapping territories. Thus females will remain in their home territories and raise their offspring in the region where they grew up.

Intelligence

It is broadly estimated that all non-human great apes are as intelligent as a five to six year old human child. However, based upon my experience with orangutans, chimps and gorillas, I will say that orangutans are the most intelligent great ape, second only to humans. Highly intelligent, orangutans have a well-developed frontal lobe cortex region in their brain. It is this they use to explore scenarios and run computer-like simulations in their minds, making them perhaps the best non-human problem-solvers in the world. They also display highly developed cognition and memory. Furthermore, as semi solitary beings, orangutans must be independent and self-sufficient in their rainforest homes. As they do not have the same social structures as the other great apes, they require a greater self-reliance and in depth knowledge of their environment in order to survive. Also orangutans are active fruit eaters who require intelligence to remember and locate the vast array of fruit and other food sources in the forest. Therefore, they have developed a special temporal-spatial memory and keen creative intelligence to survive.

From experience, I will say that gorillas are the least intelligent of the great apes. This is reflected in their diets as gorillas eat green vegetation found in their habitats. To handle this high cellulose diet they necessarily sit around and 'fart' all day as the flatulence causing vegetation is slowly digested. However, due to the fact that they have to eat so much of this low value food they also do not require such an in depth knowledge of food sources. Thus they don't have to be as intelligent. Interestingly, some anthropologists think, as a whole, humans are now less intelligent due to the impacts of the Agricultural Revolution. They explain that with more reliable food supplies, an individual could be relatively unintelligent yet still survive and successfully breed. Therefore, anthropologists suggest that humans have gone down the gorilla path in some way and lost some of our hunter-gatherer intelligence. [64]

Chimpanzee Mind

Common chimpanzees are considered as the most human-like in regards to their behaviours. As social beings, chimps and humans display shared traits ranging across the spectrum from altruistic and compassionate through to aggressive and destructive, as well as most behaviours in between. At the aggressive end of scale, chimps are capable of hostile, violent and even murderous behaviour.[65] Along with humans, they are also one of the only other species known to wage concerted and organised war on members of their own species. Like us, chimps are known to send out co-ordinated hunting parties, commit infanticide, and exhibit brutality and cruelty. [66] Again, like us they kill and eat other animals and have an omnivorous diet.

Chimps and humans also demonstrate instinctive tribal natures and are each driven by these, which means that in many ways these instincts *think us, we don't think them.* Due to this fact, our tribal hunter-gatherer imperatives for survival and our instinctive behaviours mean that we can become unconscious victims of our own biology. With the combined influences of their highly social groups and tribal nature, male chimps can form coalitions to dominate their communities, as humans do. Chimpanzee researcher Jane Goodall famously witnessed chimps at Gombe in Tanzania destroying a whole community made up of former fellow members who had moved on to form a separate group. [67] It seemed that the original community subsequently viewed the new group as a threat, so war broke out between them and over a few years most members of the separatist group were killed. Unfortunately, humans can also share the desire to destroy and inflict pain on others of our species, so we find a mirror in our close relatives the chimpanzees.

On the other hand, chimps are also known to be intelligent and inquisitive and to demonstrate loving, caring and nurturing actions such as grooming, friendship and play. They can also be co-operative and mindful of the well-being and safety of their fellow community members, and at the same time can show compassion and closeness. Researchers have observed that they cultivate and select friends of similar natures to themselves and have a sense of moral justice and fairness, to a degree. Therefore, chimps, like us, can be highly loving and supportive as well as destructive and aggressive, so we share this striking dichotomy with our chimpanzee relatives.

Orangutan Nature

In contrast to the chimp and human tribal behaviours, orangutans tend to have mild temperaments and embody, what I can only say is a noble, selfless quality. In many ways this is because with a typical upbringing in the wild, they are reared to be independent and self-sufficient individuals. Therefore, when they interact with others they do not need or want anything from them, and this is something which well adjusted, secure humans share in common with orangutans. This is not to say that orangutans do not get angry, jealous or aggressive and that I have not encountered badly behaved orangutans, because I have. Usually, though, there is a very good reason for the typically non-confrontational orangutan to exhibit aggressive behaviour. For example, females who are nursing infants or protecting their young may become defensive if they think that their offspring are being threatened; males competing for fertile females or territories; or orangutans who are under attack from predators seeking to defend or extricate themselves from a dangerous situation.

In fact, it has been recorded that humans have been attacked and injured by orangutans. This includes humans being bitten and even losing fingers, as orangutans defend themselves or attack to get food or objects. However, they won't attack to kill, because orangutans don't appear to have the internal intention or trigger to kill, even if they may want to hurt an attacker or to protect their young or their females. To me it seems that they lack the killer instinct, which we humans unfortunately display all too often.

Interestingly, across the centuries of human contact with our enigmatic orange cousins, we have been responsible for butchering at least one million of them. However, the telling fact is that, whether in the wild or in captivity, there is no record of any orangutan ever killing a human being. Even when a mother orangutan is defending her baby she will protect her offspring to her last breath in an attempt to save her young, as wild orangutans do not display the biological switch-off mechanism with their babies and will not leave them. However, she never kills the attacker, even though she can be a number of times physically stronger than a human. Instead, she steadfastly stands alone to protect her baby and will do everything within her power to avoid leaving her young. The equally remarkable fact is that adult male orangutans have canines as large and as strong as a tiger and are recognised as being up to seven times as powerful as any human being. Again, despite their physical capability, whilst they have been known to defend themselves and potentially injure an attacker to escape, they have not killed a human.

We can often see the commonalities between ourselves and our great ape cousins, sometimes in the most surprising places.

Boardroom Chimps

For evidence of our chimp-like tendencies and drives, one doesn't have to look much further than the usually male dominated corporate executive boards in most cities of the world. Below is an example from the boardroom.

As part of my work, I have been invited to give talks to corporate groups in Australia and the USA as a way of providing insight into their patterns of behaviour and ways of interacting with one another. This is because in many of these predominantly male enclaves of business and corporate governance we are basically chimpanzee coalitions in much of our conduct and deeds. By this I mean that if we understand chimpanzee social and cultural behaviour then we can predict the behaviour of corporate executives. This includes the tendency for the strongest and smartest male of the group to be undermined and have his career stymied by a coalition made up of the second, third and even fourth male chimps in the hierarchy. By combining forces, the lower ranked chimps can render the most capable male unable to reach the top position. The strongest and smartest male ultimately falling prey to the coalition of less capable chimpanzees.

This coalition also reaps the spoils of their power play by gaining access to the top spots within the group and the status this affords. The group is then led by not necessarily the best, wisest or strongest male chimps but by those who are most manipulative, political and cunning. *The rules of the game can be explained by this simple example - Chimpanzee Number Three will always support chimpanzee Number Two over chimpanzee Number One. This is because there is less power difference between Number Three and Number Two, than between Number Three and Number One. Therefore, Number Three will gain more power and influence by supporting Number Two. In this scenario, a truly talented individual working their way up a corporate ladder may find it difficult due to this in-built chimp-like behaviour. Instead they may be better off as an entrepreneur and starting their own company.*

Interestingly, a recent study has found that within work and competitive environments there appears to be a group dynamic amongst humans which tends to penalise co-operative, nice-guy, over achiever types. [68]*This means that some like to see super helpful, nice people being brought down a peg or two in status or being punished. It seems that it may just be a characteristic of human nature to be suspicious about nice people. The same researchers also suggested that this dynamic may apply to conservationists and those helping the environment. As we seek to ensure that these good people don't look too much better than everyone else.* [69]

When I explain this chimp dynamic to predominantly male groups they are generally shocked and surprised with the accuracy of the descriptions I can give them based on usual chimp behaviour. This is because most corporate board members see themselves as relatively sophisticated and intelligent individuals. However, based upon their rather chimp-like, instinct driven conduct it appears that they are more influenced by their ancient urges to dominate, reach for power and gain status.

Yet, there are other ways of applying our intellect to overcome our chimp-like nature.

Meeting the Guru

During my time at the zoo I was fortunate to meet and work with a diverse range of committed individuals. These included volunteers, docents and members of the Zoo Society who gave their time and energy to support the zoo and the animals within its care. At one stage the head of the fundraising arm of the Zoo Society was a compassionate woman who was interested in spirituality. Capable and practically minded she did not appear to be what, from my scientifically based perspective, I would term as 'airy fairy.' She also displayed an even temperament and radiated inner happiness.

Coupled with this I also had the opportunity to meet and speak with her husband. In my interactions with him I was struck by the fact that he was one of the most intellectual and consciously present people I had ever met. In fact there was something about him which made him stand out as different from many of the people I had mixed with in the work arena. Yet I had no idea that his unique presence and strength of intellect came from his study of philosophy. However this was soon to change.

One afternoon I received an invitation to attend a fundraising lecture at the zoo being given by the respected Indian Guru and scholar A. Parthasarathy. I decided to go along as I knew this couple would be there and that they highly valued the insight of Parthasarathy. The talk was to be on the Guru's acclaimed book, "Vedanta Treatise" and cover his study into spirituality. [70] Even though at this stage in my life I would not have normally been attracted to spend my time listening to a spiritual Guru, I also understood that perhaps this was an opportunity to experience something out of my usual comfort zone. My friends also assured me that this event would have both insight and research behind it. So it definitely ticked a few boxes for me and I was curious to find out for myself what it was that made this couple so refreshingly different.

I attended the talk and found the information Parthasarathy shared to be not only fascinating, but it also struck a chord within me. Reasoned, logical and yet deeply philosophical in nature, the Guru's words had touched on what I sensed to be truth. A truth which had long sat dormant within my being. At the same time as Parthasarathy spoke, I experienced the feeling that what he was saying was somehow what I had always known. However his words had made the knowledge conscious within me. This is what I have since learnt to be the 'ring or sound of truth'. Needless to say I was intrigued.

During the visit Parthasarathy made a point of approaching me. When he reached me we shook hands, I introduced myself and he began to speak. Looking directly at me he said, "Leif I recognise a greatness within you that you cannot see. Would you like to come to India and study, as I think you could benefit from the experience?" Surprised and taken aback at this sudden invitation, yet excited at the prospect, I replied, "I would love to study with you in India. However, I'm a zookeeper and don't have the funds available to do so at the moment." Parthasarathy simply smiled and nodded and went on to say, "I am inviting you to join me so money won't be an issue. I will waive all costs. Please come as my guest for six weeks." As I heard the words and comprehended their meaning I experienced a sense of inner congruence. Strangely it felt as if it was the right thing to do. I had never been to India before and certainly never imagined travelling there to spend time with a Guru. However life sometimes offers us opportunities which lead us in a direction we may not have imagined, yet take us to where we have always needed to be.

So I chose to accept this invitation and was soon bound for India.

Chapter Three
Speaking Our Language

'Who you are speaks so loudly, I cannot hear what you are saying.'
Ralph Waldo Emmerson

Another way in which we have defined ourselves as different from all other great apes is through our capacity for language. As we have both rich verbal and written forms of communication, we have perceived ourselves to be unique and considered language to be the domain of humans alone. This is not true, as all great apes also have highly developed forms of communication. However, because these means of communication are different from our own communication structures, for much of history, we have not recognised them as such. Unfortunately, this has meant that not only have we misunderstood the communication styles of great apes, we have judged them as lacking in intelligence because they don't speak our language. Perhaps, though, this could equally be perceived as humans lacking the insight and wisdom necessary to appreciate this fact and seek to learn their forms of communication ourselves?

Speaking with the Great Apes

The idea of speaking with other great apes became popular in the West during the 1960s and 1970s and early research in this area was conducted with chimpanzees. Initially, scientists attempted to teach the chimps to speak our verbal language. However, because no other great ape possesses the vocal cords required for human speech, these original trials were unsuccessful. Undeterred, researchers decided to shift their focus to another ready-made form of communication, American Sign Language (ASL), a form of hand signing used by the hearing impaired. In these new experiments, young chimpanzees, orangutans and gorillas were selected and raised almost as humans and were systematically taught sign language.

Many of these great ape participants would not only learn sign language but also begin to communicate directly with the researchers. In doing so, they were found to be highly intelligent, sophisticated beings capable of communicating with humans and amongst themselves. Many of these experiments with ASL ended when the great ape participants grew older or neared adolescence, as they were considered too strong for their human handlers. As such, some of the results recorded were akin to rating the intelligence of humans by going to a primary school and assessing the children on their knowledge and understanding of adult concepts and ideas. To a scientific way of thinking this could be perceived as a missed opportunity.

However, many of these great ape participants would go onto be recognised in scientific circles and around the world for their sign language skills. One of the most famous of these was Chantek the orangutan who I met personally and with whom I interacted in a USA-based primate facility. As recounted in my last book, once Chantek had grown to adolescence the language trials involving him were ceased. Unfortunately, he was sent back to the primate facility where he was caged and isolated in a small concrete cell for 11 years. When we first met, he immediately signed me the message, "*Get the car keys and take me home.*" Happily, I was able to assist, in a small way, with the process of having Chantek relocated to Zoo Atlanta. It was here that he was able to live out the rest of his life with space to move and the opportunity to communicate once more with humans.

Of the gorilla species, the most well-known signing great ape was Koko, who was raised and taught by Francine 'Penny' Patterson from Stanford University. Also now deceased, Koko was said to have learned over 1,000 ASL hand signs and understood many more spoken English words.[71] Koko was also famous for her love of her pet kitten and for the heart-break she experienced when her pet unexpectedly died. When asked where she thought her kitten had gone after death, Koko's response was signed as, "*Warm dark hole.*" Perhaps this is an intriguing insight into the concept of death from the perspective of a gorilla?

Instead of learning sign language, Kanzi the bonobo was taught lexigrams and symbols as a way to communicate with humans. Thought to be able to understand more of the human language than any other non-human being, he has learned a vast array of lexigrams and constructs his language exchanges with grammar and syntax.[72] In this way Kanzi is still communicating with researchers to this day.

A number of common chimpanzees have also been involved in language research such as this. Vicki, Washoe and Nim are perhaps the most well-known members of the species to have learned some form of human language and did so during the 1950s to the 1970s. A range of other chimps have also been taught sign language or been used in various human research projects over the years. As an example of the intelligence and comprehension of our chimp cousins, it was recognised amongst the sign language chimps of Washington State University that they understood the visual and seasonal cues of Christmas celebrations. To the chimps, these occasions were remembered as times of plentiful food, celebration and the appearance of decorated Christmas trees with presents under the tree for everyone. Therefore, as the weather cooled and the northern hemisphere winter season arrived, the chimps would begin signing to their keepers questions such as, "*When are the fruit and candy trees coming?*" Evidently they cognised that when it became cold, Christmas trees would come out and food and gifts would arrive. Much like the bountiful fruiting trees of their natural habitat. Therefore, they projected themselves forward in anticipation of the future event, with the full learned experience that Christmas trees came out at the same time each year.

Washoe the Compassionate Chimp

Washoe the chimp became well known for her caring and compassionate nature. Not only was she observed assisting and protecting the fellow chimps of her facility, she was also known for her compassion towards her human carers.

An example of her empathetic nature was demonstrated when one of Washoe's carers, a volunteer named Kat, became pregnant. As Kat's pregnancy progressed, Washoe was curious and often asked Kat about her baby, using the sign for "baby," to signify her understanding of this. Unfortunately, Kat suffered a miscarriage, and was absent from work for some time after the event. Upon her return to work, Kat knew that Washoe would be miffed with her as the sociable chimp didn't like her human carers to be unexpectedly absent from the facility for any length of time. Mindful of this and aware that Washoe had also lost two of her own babies, the carer signed to Washoe, "My baby died." In response, Washoe immediately looked down. When she finally looked up into Kat's eyes she slowly signed, "Cry." Then gently drew her finger down the carer's cheek as if tracing the course of tears falling down her face.[73] In that moment Kat and Washoe silently shared their joint grief and their humanity.

Saving the Signing Chimps

Compassion between humans and great apes can extend both ways, as shown in the following story of one of Washoe's researchers. In this instance, a human was able to extend compassion to his chimpanzee friends and demonstrate a greater form of humanity in action.

Washoe was originally under the care of psychologists Allen and Beatrix Gardner at the University of Nevada and later Roger and Deborah Fouts from Washington State University.[74] As mentioned earlier, when sign language research ceased, many of the great apes involved did not fare too well, with some ending up in research facilities or being returned to the organisation from which they originally came. Unfortunately, this was the case when the experiment involving Washoe and some other sign language-trained chimps was completed in the 1970s.[75] It turned out that these chimps were on loan from the US military and once the language trials were finished, the military wanted their chimps returned for research. Sadly, Washoe and her friends were destined to be trained as bomber pilots on flight simulators. This would be done to assess whether, during a nuclear war with Russia, human flight crews could continue to fly and drop their bombs over Moscow. Such testing would mean that the chimps were to be dosed with lethal levels of radiation, then studied to see if they could still fly the simulated bomber flights long enough to reach their target before becoming too ill or dying.

Having become aware of the impending fate of the much-loved Washoe and other chimps, Roger Fouts decided to do something about the situation. Taking matters into his own hands he organised a special semi-trailer and drove it to the research facility where the chimps were held awaiting their transfer back to the US military. Making his move in the middle of the night, Fouts rescued the chimps and took them to Washington State in the semi-trailer.

With the US military suing him for theft and pursuing the return of the chimps as their property, Fouts publicised the plight of Washoe and the other sign language chimps. As the general public learned about the situation, there was a massive outcry. People became galvanised on behalf of these special chimps and took action. Ultimately, Washoe and her friends were freed from the US military's 'ownership' and rehoused in a more humane location, where they were able to live out their lives protected from the threat of military experimentation. It's interesting to note with this story that humans are obviously capable of recognising and elevating the value of other sentient life forms, such as these chimps, and protecting them. However, it is when we choose to do this on an ongoing basis, as the norm rather than the exception that will make all the difference in the long term.

As we have seen, our great ape cousins have displayed the ability to learn some of our language forms, however their own communication systems are rich and varied.

Great Ape Language

Orangutans - Even though we know that orangutans do not have the vocal chords necessary to speak as we do, they do have their own well-developed form of communication. This involves body language and to a lesser extent sounds which they use when interacting closely with other orangutans. As masters of observation it is estimated that orangutans could use body language and visual communication cues for as much as 90 percent of their communication. Using these non-verbal signals to communicate, they exhibit many socially learned behaviours and cultural traditions which are passed down from generation to generation. For example, orangutans have what is referred to as a play face to let other orangutans know when they are exhibiting playful behaviour. In the young this play face is like a smile and shows their teeth but when orangutans mature to adulthood, the play face changes so that their teeth are covered. This is because, as adults, a show of teeth indicates aggressive or threatening behaviour.

Their sound vocalisations include repetitive kiss-squeaks with which they can transmit a wide range of signals through their jungle home.[76] These are often made when the orangutan is feeling stressed, fearful or under pressure. Research has shown that female orangutans will use the kiss-squeak to educate their young as to the dangers of the forest, but she will do so once the danger has passed. For example, in one study, a research team found that when a mother orangutan saw what she thought was a tiger in the vicinity of her tree, she ensured that both she and her baby remained absolutely silent. Then once the danger had passed and the tiger had moved on, she would wait for a number of minutes before using her kiss-squeak to teach her baby about the danger that had occurred. This demonstrates both a clear understanding of events over time and also the transmission of culture to her baby.[77]

Large mature males also have their signature reverberating 'long calls' which they send out into the forests to signal their presence in the environment. The 'long calls' serve a double purpose for the dominant males: Firstly, they warn other males that they are in the vicinity so they can avoid conflict and unwanted confrontation with dominant males. Secondly, these calls signal the whereabouts of the male to mature females so they can seek him out if they are in oestrus and wish to mate. Using forethought and planning, an adult male will send his long call out from his night nest during the evening before he sleeps. By sending the call in the direction he wishes to travel the next day, he gives prior warning to other males and also alerts females of his impending presence in the area.

Orangutans are more than capable of learning sign language as a means of communication with humans. We know that they can learn more than 200 words in ASL and I have observed them comprehend spoken languages such as English and Indonesian. They can also read the body language of others, including humans and are known to understand people perfectly in this way. Because of this, they can communicate with us and we can converse with them.

Chimpanzees – Chimpanzees and bonobos are far more like humans in their communication and language styles. Even though they rely heavily on body language and gestures, they are also more vocal in their communication expression. Due to their large group social dynamics, chimps necessarily need to communicate signals and messages to fellow members of their community. Their extended social groups may comprise more than 100 individuals and each group has acknowledged hierarchies amongst its members.

Chimp faces are highly animated and they also display the fear grimace, which humans have often incorrectly interpreted as a smile. Adult chimps are, in fact, demonstrating aggressive and threatening behaviour if they show their teeth in a grimace. This is used as a warning to other chimps that the sender is feeling stressed or threatened. Research suggests that chimps can convey as many as 19 different messages to each other using a range of up to 66 recognisable gestures. They are clearly able to send and receive specific signals and messages between individuals within the group.[78]

Chimpanzee young are also born with a tuft of white hair located near their coccyx. This white tuft signals to the community that the individual is still young and learning. Therefore, it provides infants and young with the freedom to do things that adults do not, such as climbing, jumping on and playing with dominant males and members of the community without censure or punishment. However, as soon as the white tuft of hair disappears, the individual chimp must now begin to obey the group and conform to strict social and cultural guidelines. They have this white tuft for only a few years, it disappears in early childhood. [79]

Gorillas - Like their chimpanzee cousins, gorillas are also highly expressive in their forms of communication and language. As social great apes, they also live in family groups of unrelated females, (harems) and use body language, gestures, full body actions, calls, sounds and even hoots to signal each other and warn off potential predators. Known to display at least 20 to 25 different sounds with specific meanings they can be both noisy and active communicators.[80]

They display laugh-like behaviour and are known to stick their tongues out when within the group. Gorillas also have good hearing capabilities and a reasonable sense of smell so they are quickly alerted if danger is near. [81] The dominant males are recognised for their forceful behaviours when under threat from other dominant or younger males. These include screaming, beating their chest and defensively charging at interlopers.

Like chimps, gorilla young also display the white tuft of hair from birth until early childhood, similarly this allows the youngsters to play, romp and climb over and around the members of their group without punishment. However, this behaviour also ceases once the young have passed the stage when the white tuft disappears.

How can we better communicate with each other as humans and perhaps extend greater humanity to our great ape cousins?

True Communication

In my years in conservation and animal welfare I have observed some excellent outcomes due to authentic communication. On the other hand, I have also observed how polarising and divisive these fields can be when persons with different ways of seeing the world interact. This is especially true when an individual's perspective becomes fixed *or ossifies*. By ossification, I refer to the situation in which a position, opinion or strategy becomes set in stone and a rigid paradigm of *right / wrong, good / bad, them / us* develops. Once this occurs within individuals, we lose our openness, ability to listen, natural fluidity of thought, willingness to learn, appreciation of another's perspective and the opportunity to co-create a viable way forward. Instead we go into opposition and even conflict with each other as we attempt to protect our position and defend our turf. This means that we have no room to move when working to find a solution to the challenges we face. From this I have learned that a more refined and balanced form of understanding is needed between us if we are to move forward. I call this *true communication*.

I think this simple Zen parable beautifully illustrates the importance of the two key aspects of true communication:

1. Being present and open in the moment to authentically communicate.
2. Emptying the mind and being willing and receptive to listen to another person to hear what they have to say.

A Cup too Full

One day, a highly educated and scholarly professor of philosophy heard of a Guru who was visiting a neighbouring town. As a world expert in his field, the professor wished to meet with the Guru as a way of expanding his knowledge in the area. He sent word to request a meeting with the spiritual master and was able to arrange a time to see him the following afternoon. The next day, the professor travelled to meet the Guru and was soon seated at a lovely table under a shady tree in the garden of the home where the Guru was staying.

Asking the professor if he would like a cup of tea, the Guru placed an empty cup on the table in front of him. He began to pour the tea from a large tea pot. As the Guru did so, the professor began asking questions. The Guru remained silent and kept pouring the tea into the cup. Soon the hot tea was overflowing from the cup and spilling onto the table beneath, yet the Guru continued to pour the tea.

Realising what was happening the professor stopped mid-sentence and asked the Guru, "What are you doing?" The Guru stopped pouring and looked at the professor and said, "I cannot teach you because you are already full to overflowing like this tea cup. There is no space within you to learn. Until you empty your mind and your heart I can't teach you anything."

As the parable demonstrates, if we are too full of our own opinions, self-importance or beliefs and only wish to expound our knowledge, we do not have the capacity to learn new information. Nor the ability to truly communicate with another person. Rather, we are unable to take on anything else as we are already overflowing. When we come from this state of being full, we are unable to understand or learn as there is no place of emptiness and openness to hear new knowledge.

For true communication to occur there are a few simple elements to consider.

Having Intention

To truly communicate with another being our intention to do so is the key. We must intend to be present and listen to another as well as express ourselves through language, and non- verbal cues. With this comes the transcendence and the feeling of oneness with another person that exists in being present, listening and sharing our thoughts.

Listening Deeply

Listening is a vital part of communication. There are two parts to the ability to listen deeply. Firstly we must stop the internal chatter of our own mind, because without doing this we are only half listening as we focus on what we wish to say, instead of listening to the other person. Secondly once the other person has spoken, we should allow some space and wait before responding to say something in return. Thus the art of truly listening is somewhat rare, as most of us struggle to take control of our thoughts to create the space to listen. Unfortunately, we will often jump in and interject before the other person has finished speaking and, therefore, do not truly listen at all.

Empathy

Another part of true communication is the quality of empathy, as without empathy for another we are not authentically listening. Interestingly, Sun Tzu states in his book, *"The Art of War,"* *"You must have empathy with your enemy, as unless you have empathy for your enemy you can't understand them and therefore can't win."*[82] In reality, empathy and true communication is the best way to avoid war, but even if an enemy turns against us, listening and feeling empathy is always the key.

For example, I have found that unless I can empathise with those who are seemingly on the opposite side of conservation, such as representatives of large corporations clearing the forest, I will not be able to understand them or make a difference in the outcome. To help me to develop empathy and forge a connection with these individuals, I always sit next to them at meetings. By having us, two individuals with different perspectives, sit alongside each other, a significant psychological impetus to co-operate is created, as is a much greater opportunity for us to agree. This is because it is our instinctual desire to belong and agree with others. Therefore, next time you sit down for a challenging discussion, sit next to the one who will most likely disagree with you. By doing so you will both be more likely to bond, agree and find a greater solution to your issues. It will also help your mind and heart to connect with the other person. In this way everyone wins.

Asking Questions

When we wish to truly communicate with another individual, we are curious and wish to ask questions of them to learn and understand. Asking open-ended questions that encourage deeper and more meaningful answers is an excellent way of seeking to understand. Open ended questions are those which one can't generally answer *"yes" or "no."* For example, who, when, how, which, where, why are all the start of these types of questions. In a meeting, I will often ask, *"How can we do this?"* Rather than focusing only the issues in front of us, because true communication always seeks to understand.

Interestingly, when I am presenting a lecture, I find that many of the people asking questions are there to make a statement, instead of to seek answers. I think this is rooted in our human need to be noticed and project our existing ideas onto others. Thus fake questions become vehicles for garnering attention instead of gaining knowledge and understanding. In these cases, the person is already full of their answers and opinions. I think Einstein said it best when he asked, *"What is my knowledge compared to my ignorance?"* By realising how little he knew, Einstein had the ability to learn, see more and grow. Conversely, if an individual sees themselves as an expert their knowledge is solidified. Being an expert is a death knell for growth and learning; a true expert knows they are ignorant and can, therefore, always gain new knowledge.

Creative Solutions

Another key for true communication is looking for the solutions, rather than focusing solely on the problem. With this comes perspective as we often think solutions will be a result of our intellect and knowledge, but the creative solution tends to come from the space between our thoughts. We sometimes reach the most creative solutions after we have almost given up and the mind temporarily stops in frustration, allowing the space for a creative solution to arise. Many artists have consciously or sub consciously discovered that the direct route to creative expression is to allow for space between the thoughts, as the creative solution comes from the emptiness and the openness to receive a solution. In this way, creativity is able to emerge from the space and seems to come out from nowhere. Therefore, in addition to using logic and thinking through a problem, we should have space in our minds to allow for clarity of thinking. In this way, we can reach a space of surrender so the creative way of thinking comes naturally with an innovative solution, art form or answer.

From a conservation point of view we need both intellectual knowledge and creativity to solve the problems we face. As humans, we have the ability to change our perspective, be open to new possibilities and to shift our point of view, because we have the intelligence and the innate capacity to do so. The following story illustrates how an experience of true communication was able to create a shift in perspective and, ultimately a different outcome for myself, a colleague and a captive orangutan.

A Shift in the Rainforest

I will always remember the journey I took with a former CEO of the zoo in which I worked and the shift which occurred between us amidst the heat, humidity and muddy terrain of an isolated Sumatran rainforest. It was one in which I experienced and witnessed transformation within and between two human beings. This is why it remains a memorable journey in my work with The Orangutan Project (TOP) to this day.

During my time as the Curator of Exotics at the Perth Zoo I was working on a ground-breaking project to release the first captive zoo-born Sumatran orangutan back into the wild. This audacious program, one which had never been attempted before, involved a female orangutan named Temara and members of the zoo's Primate Team. I was keen to get this project off the ground for a number of reasons. Firstly, it would be a way of demonstrating how appropriately raised captive born orangutans could once again live in the wild and contribute to their species' conservation. Secondly, it would give Temara, and other captive orangutans at the zoo, the opportunity to live wild and free in the natural rainforest environment for which they are perfectly adapted. Thirdly, as a way of helping people to become aware of and informed about the plight of all orangutans, both captive and in the wild. Finally, I not only intuitively knew that this was possible, but believed that it was the right thing to do. (A detailed description of our journey to release Temara can be found in my last book "Orangutans, My Cousins, My Friends" [83] and also in "Reaching for the Canopy" [84] written by fellow TOP team member and talented Primate Keeper, Kylie Bullo).

So I began to develop a plan to bring the process into reality. Initially, it was discussed amongst the team and once we were aligned with the concept, I then had to present the project to the zoo's board and CEO. It was essential that I gain not only the board's approval and support, but most importantly the CEO's, because what I was proposing was that the zoo allow me to remove and release one of their captive orangutans. In this case, Temara, a fiery female orangutan who had been born and raised within the zoo. Not only was I suggesting they free an orangutan in their possession, I was also requesting that they pay for the preparation, training, release and monitoring costs involved. Mindful of this and the fact that zoo management and I did not always agree or share the same opinions, I made my submission to the board.

A strong minded organisational manager, the CEO listened to the proposal with initial curiosity. And it did take some discussion and persuasion on our team's behalf to have the idea considered. However, to the credit of the CEO at the time, she could appreciate the benefit of the project and finally came around to seriously considering going ahead with the plan. After some of her original concerns were resolved, the CEO tentatively approved the plan to free Temara, however, there was one provision. She wanted to personally visit the proposed release site in Sumatra before the project commenced and hopefully have the chance to see orangutans in their natural habitat. To my mind, this was a great *suggestion as it would enable her to understand the conditions into which Temara would be released and also ensure that she had a good handle on the scope of the process as a whole. In addition, she was going to be responsible for providing the funds and the team required for the unique project so professionally this was her version of due diligence.*

However, logistically it meant that the CEO would have to make the challenging journey to the remote and isolated rainforest jungle of the Bukit Tigapuluh (BTP) release site in Jambi, Sumatra. This was not an easy nor a brief trip to make. In fact, it was an arduous and challenging one. It also had the added factor of the region's hot, humid climate to consider. Basically it involved a number of flights by international and domestic air to reach the region in Sumatra. From the small regional airport there was travel by road to the general area followed by an often gruelling journey in specially modified four wheel drive vehicles along muddy, undulating and inhospitable unsealed jungle tracks. These tracks had the unenviable reputation of being some of the most difficult to traverse in the region and even the rugged four wheel drive vehicles regularly become bogged in the thick, wet rainforest mud. Additionally, once we had travelled as far as we could within the BTP ecosystem, there was no way to reliably see released orangutans other than by making the demanding trek by foot through the hilly, dense jungle environment. This had to be done whilst carrying our own supplies and backpack. In short, the journey was physically and mentally testing and not to be taken lightly.

In addition to the rigorous nature of the trip as a whole, the CEO was not naturally an outdoor type of person. As a business career professional who was more accustomed to tailored suits and the demands of the office environment in which she worked, her fitness levels were not exceptionally high. As I had already taken a number of these journeys during my time in the rescue and release of orangutans in the region and had personally experienced how demanding they could be, I explained this aspect of the trip to her in detail. Aware and

68

mindful of what she would encounter, the CEO was still committed to visiting the release site. I appreciated this commitment as it would be her determination to do so which would ultimately govern whether or not we received the green light for the project. Thus, the trip was arranged and we were scheduled to take the journey together to view Temara's new home.

Setting off on our ten day trip, we met at the airport. To some observers, it may have appeared that we were the classic odd couple, with me suitably dressed for the role of the hippy conservationist and the CEO, as always, looking professional and well-presented, complete with make-up and hair styled for our long expedition. However, the time we were able to spend in each other's company during the different stages of the trip was significant for a number of reasons. Firstly, we were able to view each other as persons outside the confines of the zoo environment where we worked, with our roles to fulfil and parts to play within the system. Secondly, we were able to share our ideas, listen to each other's perspectives and genuinely hear what the other said. I think that it is true to say that the journey itself is perhaps more important than the destination. This is something we experienced as we progressed through our trip to the rainforest together.

Finally, after a couple of days of fairly constant and trying travel, we arrived at the BTP station where we would stay overnight before making the trek to see the orangutans. Agreeing to meet early in the morning for the trek, we went through some last preparations and retired to our separate quarters for the night. The following morning, we met up in the cool early morning air of the rain forest. The CEO was well dressed for the trek, still maintaining her immaculate make-up and hair style. For this challenging four- hour trek we were accompanied by project manager Peter Pratje from the Frankfurt Zoological Society. We set off as soon as possible in an attempt to avoid the inevitable jungle heat, stifling humidity and active insect life that became more invasive as the day wore on. Due to the remote location of the site, it was tough going. We had to trek through dense forest, along over grown trails and difficult terrain. It was hot, it was humid, yet all the while we were surrounded by the intense, raw beauty of the jungle.

After approximately three hours of trekking we saw some movement in the lush canopy above us and caught a glimpse of the signature orange flash of a Sumatran orangutan. I turned slowly to the CEO and silently signalled for her to look up into the trees where the orangutan was feeding. She stopped in her tracks and turned her eyes upward. We all stood together in silence, filled with awe at the sight of this majestic, free orangutan peacefully feeding in the rainforest canopy above. For what seemed like an extended moment in time, we were able to appreciate the wonder and beauty of the experience we were sharing with this wild sentient being. Finally, as the orangutan moved further into the forest in search of more food, the CEO and I simply stood in mute recognition of what had just occurred. In that moment, exhausted, hot, drenched in sweat and with the remnants of her make-up streaming down her face, the CEO turned to me with glistening eyes and said, "I get it Leif. I understand now what you have been trying to tell me. Thank you for helping me to experience this."

I still recall the effect of those words that I heard in the jungle all those years ago and remember the truth with which they resonated between us. Something had shifted within and between both the CEO and I. It was a transformational - and some would say transcendent moment - for both of us. We as two humans could gain a shared glimpse into the world of our orangutan friends and experience the truth that we are each connected, we each matter and we are each sentient persons. Such a moment is all it takes for minds to change, hearts to open and for this shift in seeing to occur. A shift which provides the knowledge that all human beings have the capacity to see into the world of another.

I often recount this story when I speak around the world and as I conduct eco tours into the rainforest habitats of the orangutans. I am happy to say that over the years I have been lucky enough to hear these same words uttered by people from different parts of the globe. No matter what the language, the message is invariably the same: they get it, they understand and they see things differently. At some point in their journey, they come to appreciate the gift of moments such as these.

And what of Temara and her journey to freedom? After our trip to the rainforest, the CEO gave her full support to the project to release Temara. Over time we were able to successfully prepare, train and release this intelligent orangutan back into the protected rainforest of the BTP ecosystem in Sumatra. Happily, the program continued even after I left the zoo and other captive orangutans were also able to be released back into the wild. All thanks to the ability of humans to change their perspectives.

Section Two
How We Think

'The world as we have created it is a process of our thinking.
It cannot be changed without changing our thinking.'
Albert Einstein

The next stage on our journey to *finding our humanity* is an inner one in which we explore some of our basic psychology. This means our first task must be to look within ourselves and become aware of our internal landscape and habitual thinking structures, because if we truly wish to see a shift in the outer world, we must first cultivate a shift within ourselves. As when we are blind to the influences of our biological drives, instinctive behaviours and cultural programming, our thinking can become imbalanced. When this is the case, these innate drives *think us, instead of us thinking them* and we remain generally unconscious of the fact. Therefore, we need to restore the balance in our thinking and in our society to solve the problems of our times. By bringing greater balance and integration into our inner world, we are more able to express this internal harmony in the external world and share this outwards, to others. Correspondingly, it is a natural progression to bring the equilibrium of a more balanced inner perspective into our thinking. In this way everyone benefits, ourselves included.

Chapter Four
It's All About You

'Your mission will become clear only when you can look into your own heart. Who looks outside, dreams; who looks inside, awakes.'
Carl Jung

Humanity Begins with You

As demonstrated in preceding chapters, humanity is not defined by our biology alone. Nor limited to our human nature or culture, or determined by human language and other forms of communication. Humanity is a much deeper concept than is encompassed by these traditional sign posts of our understanding. Instead, humanity is demonstrated in the proactive qualities of compassion, benevolence, empathy, kindness, understanding, tolerance and gentleness, applied with wisdom and balanced thinking. Yet to extend this wider definition of humanity with and towards other living beings we must first find it in ourselves, as how can we give something away if it is lacking within our own being? In this way, humanity begins with you and your willingness to look within. You cannot reform the world nor find your humanity unless you first reform yourself. Therefore it is through the inner journey that we can each come to see that it does not end there, and this opens us up to greater possibility for us all.

Why Look Within?

As human beings, we have different aspects of our inner world, making up our mind and consciousness. Famous Swiss psychologist Carl Jung, determined that we have a conscious, subconscious and collective unconscious mind. He equated our ego-self with the conscious mind. It contains all of the thoughts, memories and emotions of which we are aware, and our personality.[85] The unconscious mind holds those memories, pieces of information and repressed thoughts that lie hidden within our unconscious. Jung also posited the idea of a collective unconscious across human-kind which relates to our jointly developed instinctive and evolutionary past. [86] Some Eastern philosophical traditions suggest that we have a small "s" ego-based *self*, a thoughtful intellect and a greater "S" higher *Self* which connects us to a greater consciousness. Whilst modern neuroscience tells us that we have three levels of the brain-mind which cover the following:

The first level is the medulla or reactive and instinctive mind, which manages our basic drives and our ego.

The second level is the sub cortical area which stores and processes our emotions and memories.

The third level is located in the cortex region and is responsible for our self-awareness, problem solving, creative thinking and beliefs.[87]

Whichever way you choose to consider and explore your mind, your thought processes and your consciousness is up to you, as I am neither a psychologist nor a neuroscientist. Additionally, it is not my role to be prescriptive or suggest any particular path for you to take. Rather, I will point out that for millennia, humans have been interested in our inner world and the role that the mind and our consciousness plays in how we see, think and behave. As we demonstrate a range of instinct, emotion, thought and aspirational based aspects that affect our behaviours and success in life. Importantly, just because we may not be aware of them, this does not mean that they will not affect us, on the contrary, they do.

Therefore, it is valuable to embark on the inner journey to become more mindful of our internal landscape and its effects upon our choices. It is also important to learn how we can understand ourselves personally and transcend the instinctive and culturally determined aspects which make us human. Furthermore, if we do not transcend our current thinking patterns and behaviours as a species, we will continue down our current path of destroying the environment and other living beings. This we know is unsustainable. We also know that the biological and tribal imperatives out of which we are still operating are based upon our hunter-gatherer tribal past - a past which was built on being successful in small tribes on the wide plains of the savannah. However, the Agricultural Revolution first massively changed our population growth around 12,000 years ago. Subsequently the Industrial Revolution of approximately 200 years ago meant that we could alter our environment on a large-scale basis and at a rapid pace. This meant that our population size and our environment have both drastically changed, whilst our culture and behaviour has lagged behind. We need therefore to question whether we are acting at a lower level of thinking, to see this, examine it and transcend it.

Accordingly, our task becomes to look within. As the outer world is a manifestation of the inner world, so the problem lies with us. This means that if we set our inner world in order, then this will ultimately manifest in the external world in the form of better outcomes for all. The good news is that balance is a natural state and we can restore the balance and harmony in our thinking if we come to know ourselves. However, humans often try to do things in reverse. Instead, we run around attempting to find happiness and a balanced life in the outside world without ever first looking within. Even to the point that many of us may die never finding this elusive state because we have been brainwashed to seek it outside ourselves. Yet happiness is found within us and is not attached to the outer world.

How do we begin to look within?

In my experience, we generally need someone from outside our usual sphere to point the way to us. This is the traditional role of the 'Guru.' In modern times this can equate to a mentor, a master or someone who has already trodden the path and knows the way ahead. However we must like and respect this individual so that when they bring something to our attention, and into the light of our awareness, we will address it, not reject it. This is how it was for me as I began my inner journey.

Journey to India

The scant instructions for my journey were that I was to meet Parthasarathy at his ashram in a small town near Pune, West India. To get there I was to first fly to Bombay, and Parthasarathy would arrange for someone to meet me at the airport and assist me with the next part of the journey. There I was on a flight out of Perth, travelling alone to an Indian ashram in the countryside of rural India. Nothing could have prepared me for the all-encompassing sensory onslaught of this country nor for the experiences I would soon have.

Getting off the plane in the humid Bombay evening air, I was first greeted by the exotic sights, sounds and smells of this bustling city airport. Hot, dirty and teaming with people it was a scene which was difficult to take in all at once. As I came out of customs I began to look for the person who would be there to meet me. Amongst the masses of people congregated around the arrivals doors, I saw a middle aged man holding up a copy of Parthasarathy's book, "Vedanta Treatise." Relieved I had found my ride, I walked toward him and said, "Hello." He smiled a mute welcome which indicated that he didn't speak English and then motioned for me to follow him. Making our way through the crowds we exited the airport buildings and got into an old car. As we drove in silence through the city I was amazed at what I saw.

There were masses of people everywhere. People were on the street, scooters, bikes and cars rushed by with their lights off in the barely organized chaos of traffic. It was a shock for me coming from the neat, clean, quiet suburban streets of Perth, Western Australia and even my time growing up in the metropolis of Hong Kong was nothing compared to the sensory overload of Bombay. We drove for a time through increasingly squalid streets and finally arrived at an old building. I was shown to an aged couch in a second floor office which would be my makeshift bed for the night.

Early the next morning I was driven to Victoria Train Station where I would have to somehow find the correct train for the next part of my journey. If I had thought the night before was an eye opening introduction to the city, Victoria Station was a whole new level. There were beggars and homeless people sleeping on the pavement and in any available crevice or corner. People were defecating in between the train tracks, the stench of which assaulted the air. Others were waking, eating or massed on the platforms awaiting the outgoing trains. The sight of poverty was ever present. Amidst this sea of humanity I had to try and find the right platform and train by using my flimsy printed ticket as a guide. Finally locating the correct platform, I boarded an old train which was jam-packed with people. There I would stay, wedged up against my backpack, the worn and battered seat and my fellow passengers. It would take me two train journeys and a long walk before I arrived at my destination, the ashram and to see my Guru.

Without a doubt the journey to the ashram itself was an awakening of sorts and a surreal experience. I was travelling alone in this strange developing country, with its remnants of British colonial rule and the totally immersive ordered chaos of the Indian sub-continent. Even with my background of travelling in South East Asia, I can confidently say that you haven't seen the depths of poverty until you go to India. It is ever present and it can be confronting. As I would come to know, for us to grow, learn and fully develop our inner selves we sometimes have to go through challenges. By doing so we step out of our comfort zone and are then able to learn something new and of greater value. In this way we receive the benefits of something good coming out of something difficult. However, if we just cruise along the journey and it is too easy we won't get there or push ourselves to that place which offers us something higher, something of worth. Instead we must go through the challenge to gain the benefits it offers and we must do it ourselves

Life at the ashram was a regular and constant process of study, reflection and work. We would all sleep in traditional dormitories separated out into men and women's blocks. Arising at 4 am in the soft cool of the morning light to chant, we then did personal study and afterwards met for breakfast. All of the food was delicious vegetarian fare. We were also assigned to do karma yoga which meant that we worked within the ashram or around the grounds. There were regular lectures and discussion groups as well as quiet study, contemplation and mediation. We also had opportunities to meet with Parthasarathy, ask questions and gain further insight. I was told it was a very traditional schedule by Indian standards and during my time there I was just one of the crew and part of the daily routine.

At the deeper level for me this time was an inner process of widening my understanding about true education and spiritual teaching. Here the role of the Guru is one of bringing out of the student that which they already know. As it is considered that we unconsciously know the truth and that we have always known it. Therefore, the learning process for the student is an intellectual discovery of the truth and wisdom which resides deep within us all. Coming from the West and its more *instructional and directed approach to study, I found the learning environment at the ashram refreshingly different*

Almost as a confirmation that I was on the right path, one afternoon as I was reading "In the Woods of God Realization" by Rama Tirtha, the book seemed to vibrate in my hands with its depth and wisdom. [88] *Momentarily I stopped reading to consider a point of truth and glanced out of the window of my dormitory. Immediately I noticed a Northern Palm Squirrel, which were native to this area, dart across the lawn and scamper lightly up a tree. I smiled to myself at the sight of this exuberant little being, a being with which I was intimately familiar. As these character filled squirrels ran free and wild around the grounds of the zoo and I would see them on a daily basis at work. An exotic import which had been released into the grounds and learnt to live in their own communities, they were much loved members of the zoo's animal life. As I sat and watched in wonder suddenly I felt a sense of oneness and intuitively knew that I was in the right place.*

Arriving back home after six weeks, I continued with the process to know my inner self and the truth which lies within us all. Which meant I read widely in the area of philosophy and spiritual thought as well as kept up the regular practice of inner presence and contemplation. It was a constant revealing, unfoldment and learning journey as my daily routine returned to my work at the zoo and with my beloved orangutans. This gentle unveiling would continue for me into the future. As Parthasarathy would say, self-realized spiritual masters have unique experiences, often with huge life shifting moments of enlightenment. Whereas simple mortals such as I live our lives as a constant unfoldment of truth. I felt I had somehow found my path for now but it wasn't the last time I would visit India.

During my time with the Guru in India, I came to learn that some of the simplest lessons are also the most important. Within the clear-cut minimalism of simplicity lies a great depth and purity of truth. I recall that one day during a lecture, the Guru introduced the idea that there was a first duty in life for all of us. My curiosity was sparked, I thought that I was about to hear the key to the meaning of life. I recall shifting my position as I sat on the floor of the lecture hall, leaning forwards so as to catch the wisdom that I was about to hear. The Guru paused and then said, *"Our first duty in life is to be cheerful."* That was it, to-be-cheerful. At the time, I didn't think that this was particularly ground-breaking. However, the Guru went on to explain the deeper meaning of this single principle and its greater wisdom began to unfold, both for its implications for my own life, and as the lives of human beings as a whole.

Be Cheerful

'Very little is needed to make a happy life; it is all within yourself, in your way of thinking.'
Marcus Aurelius

To be cheerful is to be inwardly happy and of good spirit. If we can take this essence of happiness and good cheer with us into the world and maintain it, no matter what, we will be contributing to the greater good of all. Doing so means that we do not take our inner fears, anxieties and insecurities, past hurts, anger or disappointments and project them onto others. Rather, we must recognise these, bring them to our awareness and transcend them within ourselves. Likewise we must also identify when we are driven by biological instinct and cultural imperatives. Therefore, we need to reform ourselves inwardly first as happiness and cheerfulness reside internally, not externally. Once we have done this we can naturally and effortlessly share what is within us, with others. Thus we can be truly good and do truly good work in the external world, acting from our core of cheerfulness and love, of which we are.

It follows that if we are happy we want others to be happy also. In this way happiness is spread everywhere we go and to all with whom we interact. For example, I remember during my time in India that I was invited to attend three weddings in two days by some of the people with whom I was staying. Those celebrating the happy events were so over joyed and exuberant with the opportunity to celebrate the occasion that they naturally wished everyone around them to join in the fun and festivities. Their happiness was contagious and filled with a good will and generosity of spirit which was palpable. I could not help but be happy in their presence because cheerfulness expands to create further cheerfulness.

On the other hand, if we are in pain within ourselves the same is true. People who are unhappy have a way of making others unhappy, as they unconsciously seek to hurt others and bring them down to their level of suffering. It can only be the natural expression and extension of what is within us is manifested in our own lives and the lives of those around us. The saying, "*As within so without*," explains this perfectly. For example, can you imagine a member of an extremist terror cell who is intent on maiming and killing others, being filled with love and goodwill for all living beings, and then proceed to plan how to blow up as many people as possible? It would not happen: it is the pain, anger, suffering and hate dwelling within the terrorist that seeks expression in the outside world. Their resulting work can only be to cause pain and suffering in others.

Looking Outside Ourselves

Correspondingly it also means if we are not happy within ourselves we tend to seek happiness in the external world. This means we are driven by the attractions of the outer world such as the achievement of power, fame, reputation and money. However, to take action based on the desire to attain these things to make ourselves feel better will only result in creating short term, ineffectual outcomes. This is true in all areas of our lives. For example, if we aim to pursue money over all else, cutting corners and involving ourselves in short-term, get-rich- quick schemes, usually our original investment is lost. Alternatively, when we seek fame and power and disregard our relationships, family or health, ultimately our relationships and health falter under the pressure and lack of care. Sometimes individuals create a crisis in their lives so they are impelled to redress the imbalance. This may result in them losing everything and having to start again more wisely. We all know stories of these situations playing out in the lives of those who concentrate on the transitory external world at the cost of lasting, long term legacy. Sometimes these stories occur within our own lives.

This type of behaviour can also be observed in the field of conservation. Unreformed or unhappy individuals can fall into the cult of the environmental martyr, which is a concept I discussed in my last book. Basically in this dynamic, seemingly well-meaning people who seek to do good work in conservation, but have an underlying drive to gain external recognition in return for their efforts, tend to sacrifice themselves and burn out on the individual level. At the larger end of the spectrum within their organisations, they tend to build unsustainable structures and take ineffective measures, which lack stability and foundation, much like a house of cards. That is, what they do ultimately attracts drama and struggle and produces neither longevity nor legacy because its basis is unsound. Therefore, their efforts ultimately collapse. This can be the case even if they are not consciously aware of what they are doing, as their work becomes more about themselves than about the greater good of the whole.

Indeed, those who go out to help in conservation and animal welfare without reforming themselves inwardly, will generally encounter issues. They will tend to fight with others and cause more problems than solutions. All because they are trying to fill a void within by seeking recognition and position in the outer world. Unfortunately this is often reflected on conservation and animal welfare social media sites. Here heart-felt vitriol can be aimed at other environmental advocates and conservation organisations, creating unnecessary and damaging conflict between organisations that could be working together for a common cause.

Therefore, if inner happiness is not our first aim, aggression and harshness can lurk even within seemingly compassionate individuals. This is because a hero needs a villain in order to be seen as an altruist and to be deemed important. Thus when a fellow advocate or activist of a rival organisation is directly interfering with these people's need for power, fame, reputation or money, the chimpanzee nature can arise, leading people to attack one another. Ultimately, for the unhappy this is far closer to home than the cause they are fighting for. However, it is so unnecessary and can be avoided if we each take responsibility for our inner happiness and go beyond our instinctive chimpanzee reactions.

As a point of clarification, I will say here that there is nothing wrong with using either power, fame, reputation or money to help a worthy cause. In fact there can be great benefits in doing so and what better way to assist other living beings by using them as tools to extend compassion? However to a truly happy person, these pursuits of the external world hold no more value than old childhood toys. Toys which once seemed so important but have been left behind as the individual grows up and moves to mature pursuits.

This is why our first duty in life is to be cheerful and also why it is important to reform ourselves while we seek to reform the external conditions of the world. This takes a willingness and commitment to undertake the inner journey required to truly know oneself. The good news is that this journey is available for us now and it always has been. We do not need to chart a new path or reinvent the process, as we always have free and easy access to it. However, we must go within to rise above our conditioned and culture-based behaviours and instincts to be more humane and wiser. In this way we can access our humanity for ourselves and for all living beings.

'You believe happiness resides in the world at large.
You look for it everywhere.
Extroverted pursuits have never succeeded in finding happiness.
For happiness lies within your own person.'
A. Parthasarathy

By maintaining our inner sense of cheerfulness and clarity we can better navigate the business and organisational worlds in which we live, as illustrated in this story below.

Navigating the Boardroom

I was on the corporate executive of an organisation and in many ways the members were much like chimpanzees in their approach and behaviour. There were instances of lobbying, underhanded conflict and regular differences of opinion and position. This was a fascinating scenario to be a part of for someone like me who was interested in primate culture and social structures. As a member, I would attend meetings and we would discuss some policy or initiative. I would usually contribute to the discussion. Sometimes advocating in opposition to the general consensus if I felt that this was the right way to go. During one such meeting I had come in with a particular point of view on the issue at hand. However, after hearing some additional information and ideas on how the proposal could work, I altered my position. This changed how I would vote and I agreed with the board that they should proceed with their initiative.

Immediately after I shared my newly considered point of view, a male member of the group stood and pointed at me saying, "Look! He's changed his position. He's changed his position!" Surprised by his reaction, I looked at my male colleague to gauge the reason for his outburst. Judging by the look of victory and glee upon his face, it was as if he had finally caught me out in some way. It seemed that my change of mind was evidence that I was fallible and weak. However, to my mind, I had received further information that had helped me to make a better decision. This seemed a natural and wise thing to do in this situation. As such, I was happy to change my mind on this occasion and had no issues in doing so.

Yet the other male in the group had seen this as an opportunity to try to embarrass and demean me for my change of mind as if it was a sign of weakness. This meant we were of opposite ends of understanding regarding this issue. I considered the willingness and ability to change one's mind when presented with better information as a demonstration of intelligence and wisdom. But in the corporate chimp world it was considered a weakness instead of a strength because ego governs the group and everyone is attached to their position and their place in the hierarchy. This type of environment can stifle true communication, creativity and wise action.

Another aspect of this chimp-like attack was that it was designed to reduce my social standing within the group. Insecure people do this to make themselves feel more important, as reflected in the behaviour of lower ranked chimps jockeying for a higher position in the group.

The point here is that real strength lies in maintaining an inner balance and sense of calm cheerfulness. In doing this we can change our minds and avoid becoming stuck on defending our position or opinion, thus avoiding a descent into conflict and aggression and keeping our inner clarity. There is strength in shifting our thinking, changing our positions and moving on. In fact, we need to do this to grow, learn and evolve as humans but it is often considered a weakness by those with a chimp-like mentality.

However, if we can move past this there can be a new definition of strength and leadership, where the leader doesn't have to be right all the time. Importantly, leaders can change their minds and move in a different direction if need be. In this definition of strength, the ego is not attached to our original ideas, so our sense of self-worth is not driven by a desire to be seen as the expert in our field. Therefore we have the capacity to say, "I'm wrong," or to alter our perspective once we have received new information that refutes our earlier stance. This in turn, allows us to transcend our egos and instinctive behaviours and demonstrate greater humanity.

It is also important to mention that we should not jump to criticise another person's past actions or beliefs. In doing so, we only force the person to harden in their position and resist change to protect their sense of self-worth. Criticising others makes the person doing the criticising feel better about themselves because inherent in criticism is the idea that you are somehow superior to another. However, it has little value in effecting meaningful change in the world. It is best to be mindful of our willingness to be both kind and compassionate to ourselves as well as others.

Due to the nature of the work I do, I am often asked, *"How do you deal with all the suffering you see in your work?"* My answer is based on the following concepts:

Pain is Inevitable; Suffering is Optional

The Buddha is quoted as saying that, "*Pain is inevitable, yet suffering is optional in life*." What this means is that at some stages in our lives we will feel sadness, hurt, loss, grief, fearfulness and discomfort. This is the physical human condition; it is unavoidable. We will each experience challenges along life's path. The key is to acknowledge the pain and embrace it, instead of resisting it, so we can fully experience the event. Pain is a sign from the body and mind that we are hurt, grieving or experiencing loss. This is natural, it is human and common amongst sentient beings. However, we experience suffering to the degree to which we attempt to resist, avoid or deny that pain. Such attempts only prolong the pain and bring with it greater suffering, causing a cycle of pain and suffering for the individual trying to escape their hurt.

Instead, our task must be to feel and experience the pain, deeply and completely. Allowing the emotions to come and the tears to flow as they will. In this way, when we do not resist the pain, it passes through us and can be released and let go of against a background of inner peace. By following this process over time, we are once again free to experience love and joy, as we are free of suffering.

There is a paradox to pain, because to relieve ourselves of it we must first feel it, embrace it, release and transcend it. If we can do this, although we will experience the pain, it will be short lived and we will suffer less. In modern times humans are taught that pain is bad. However, it is neither good nor bad, it simply is. Moreover when we are prepared to feel it, we diminish it and it passes. Instead, we are now often told to avoid it at all costs, and we use medications, drugs and other addictions to mask the pain over long periods of time. This only extends and expands our suffering, because if we never experience the pain in the first place and continue to suppress it, it will never leave us. For example, people are often prescribed anti-depressants following the loss of a loved one in order to ease the grief and pain of their loss. However, grief is a natural part of the healing process and the longer they take the medication, the longer the grief remains unexpressed within their psyches. This prevents them from fully going through the healing process, causing greater long term suffering. I am not saying that anti-depressants are not necessary in some instances. Rather, I am saying that they cannot replace the natural grieving and healing process and ultimately cannot heal pain. Medication can only relieve pain for the time being, as at some stage the hurt must be released.

It is also important to note that although pain is inevitable, we are not our pain. This is why, it is vital to not *become* that sadness, illness, grief or challenging situation. Those things are not us because we are something far greater than the pain, issues and challenges; we are ourselves. Furthermore, if we have begun our inner journey and chosen to be cheerful, regardless of circumstances, we can use this as our habitual approach to the world. Then, if for some reason we are experiencing difficulty, we will do our best not to spread our sadness and lay it upon others. Instead, we will aim to maintain a cheerful, balanced disposition and help others in this manner. All resulting in a greater experience of our true humanity both within and without.

Questioning Assumptions

Over the years I have had the privilege of working with and supporting a number of excellent conservation and animal welfare organisations on the ground in Indonesia. One of these is the Centre for Orangutan Protection (COP). COP is a direct action group of focused, proactive Indonesians who campaign and act to bring an end to the destruction of the country's rainforests and the ongoing slaughter of orangutans. Whilst working to solve the cause of the problems faced in the protection of the three orangutan species, they also conduct numerous rescues of individual captive orangutans. Importantly COP also works to empower the local communities in the regions where orangutans still survive in the wild as they are the best people to protect the rainforest for the long-term. The rainforests where the orangutans live also supply these communities with food, water and their livelihoods, so it is mutually beneficial for all parties to work together.

Based in Jakarta, COP has a training school for young Indonesians where they learn about the environment and the importance of conserving and protecting the last remaining rainforest areas in the country. Interestingly, over time I had been asked to talk at this school on a number of occasions. However, I had purposely avoided taking up this invitation as I had assumed that I could be making a greater difference for orangutans elsewhere. Then one year I decided to take up the opportunity to speak at the COP school. I discovered that my assumptions were entirely incorrect and it was an amazing experience, both professionally and personally.

Amongst other things, I met a wonderful group of young educated Indonesians who cared deeply about the environment and the plight of the orangutans. What's more, they sincerely wanted to help the cause in whatever way they could without attachment to reward or recognition. I was inspired by this enthusiastic group of young people. Meeting these students reflected my own commitment to the cause and reassured me that there was a good chance we could succeed, especially with this aware and proactive group of up and coming young individuals. I could see in them the same love and respect for the orangutans and we were all working to maintain the eco systems and habitat so important to the survival of our orange cousins. It was almost as if there was an awakening amongst this younger generation and they genuinely cared about the future for their country and its endangered wildlife.

What struck me from this meeting was that the students seemed to come from the growing middle class within the country. I have seen that, in general, often the poor are too busy just making a living and trying to survive. Whilst the extremely wealthy within society have the split challenge of how and where they make their money, which is often at the expense of the environment and wildlife, creating cognitive dissonance. However, the educated, aware and mobile middle class now seemed to be the new agents for change as they had the relative freedom of time and choice to make a difference. This made sense to me because this movement within the middle classes goes back to the Agricultural Revolution, where arts, culture and thinking can flourish and spread once people can pull themselves out of survival mode and subsistence. At the same time, these individuals are still not addicted to, captivated or enamoured by power and wealth, so they have true agency as advocates for positive change. It was refreshing and inspiring to be in the company of such a similarly aligned and good-hearted group of young people.

After my talk at COP, a group of the students and I went out with a few conservationist friends to do some sightseeing. As part of this we went to a Buddhist temple in Jogjakarta where we visited the holy site and explored the area. Afterwards we all simply lay on the grass in front of the temple, within the surrounding gardens. It was a warm and balmy afternoon and as we lay together under the blue sky in silence, we each appreciated the awe and beauty of which we were part. I had a sense that we were all working for the same aim, to save and protect the orangutans yet were still able to share this silence together. It was an experience of inner and outer unity and a true reflection of our shared humanity. It was a special moment and one which would remind me to avoid making assumptions in the future.

Chapter Five
Thinking with Both the Heart and the Head

'The mind is everything. What you think you become.'
Buddha

When we consider how we think, we usually associate it with our brain or mind. However, I have found one of the most powerful shifts we can make to our way of thinking is to balance the reason of the intellect with the compassion of the heart. By doing so, we give ourselves the best opportunity to approach life with a broader, more considered perspective, one which provides greater poise, stability and a longer term view into the future. The combined wisdom of the head and the loving kindness of the heart work as two wings of the bird, functioning seamlessly together to create better outcomes in all areas of our lives. Furthermore, as the metaphor of the bird in flight implies, by using both the head and the heart in unison, our thoughts lift upwards and we begin to think and act from a higher, lighter state of being.

Interestingly, the process of embracing this new way of thinking means we do not have to give up anything. Rather, we simply become more aware of the aspect of our thinking selves which has been underutilised in our habitual thought processes. This is because many of us tend to operate from either a head-dominant or heart-dominant perspective in our thinking. With my scientific training and background, I tended to be head-dominant. However, by establishing balance between these two modalities, I was able to experience a more inclusive, expansive perspective. This, is turn, provided greater depth to my inner world and ultimately facilitated more favourable outcomes as I progressed with my work to found and build The Orangutan Project.

What is it to balance our thinking with both the head and the heart?

Way of the Head

To think with the clarity and reason of the head has been prized by scholars, scientists, mathematicians and philosophers across history. So valued has human logic and reason been in modern times that there was a period within eighteenth century Europe called the 'Age of Reason.' A time which promoted the superiority of reason over belief, superstition and myth. For the gift of the human mind bestows both the ability to learn new knowledge and skills as well as the capacity to apply what we know to identify problems, understand issues and devise a practical course of action. The intellect offers the facility to analyse specific situations and to objectively deduce what is objective truth from irrational fiction. In fact, it has been our capacity as humans to use our reasoning minds that has enabled us to survive and expand as a species. It is clear to see there are obvious advantages of using our intellect in making decisions and navigating the complex world in which we live.

Additionally, as discussed in Chapter One, biologically humans possess an extensively developed brain with large prefrontal cortex which functions in the areas of planning, cognition, problem solving and decision making. Neuroscientists now estimate there are approximately 86 billion neurons in the human brain, as well as countless more neural cells known as glial cells. [89] Studies into the purpose of glial cells are ongoing, but results seem to suggest they may govern neural function and health as well as our creativity, imagination and ability to understand abstract concepts and ideas. It is also estimated that, as thinking beings, we process anywhere from 12,000 to 60,000 thoughts per day. [90] This is a considerable amount of human brain power dedicated to thinking. It appears that we are habitually using our minds to reflect, analyse information, make decisions, recall memories, apply reason and make sense of the world. In fact, we are built for it. No doubt, the field of study into the physical brain as well as human intelligence and intellect will continue to make further break throughs into the human thought processes into the future.

Even though there are undoubtedly great benefits provided by the logic and reason of the head, to base all of our decisions and strategies for the future solely upon this can result in a cold brutality if not tempered by the compassion of the heart. This is because, when we think with the head alone a hard-edged arrogance of the mind can arise which evaluates and reduces living beings, events and ideas to data driven, fact-based statistics as a priority. In this case, we can limit ourselves with reductionist thinking paradigms of right/wrong, them/us, good/bad and black/white. Unfortunately, these ways of thinking can result in the rigid dogmas and doctrines such as fascism, communism, extremism and even economic expansionism at any cost. Each of these destroys the rights, liberties and the lives of individuals and other living beings in the quest for the perfect state, society or economic solution. To approach life through this simplistic, right/ wrong paradigm means that our thinking lacks the benefits of the discernment of the heart and the wisdom of human kindness. As such, the strength of the intellect is best applied in combination with the compassion of the heart, instead of in isolation. Below I share a story from my time at the zoo in which the cold reason of the head held sway over the empathy of the heart.

A Choice to Euthanise

In my early years as a zookeeper I was assigned to the Primate Section at Perth Zoo. Delighted to be working with such fascinating beings, I felt privileged to care for the intelligent and lively primates in this section. These included a range of monkeys, gibbons, chimps and orangutans to name a few. Over my time there I came to know these beings as unique and highly inquisitive, with distinctive characters and personalities of their own. Also, as a zookeeper, I saw it was my role, and that of the zoo for which I worked, to put the welfare of the animals first- particularly when it came to making decisions regarding their physical health and mental well-being. However, I recall a traumatic incident that helped me to see my assumption was not necessarily correct, as the managerial side of the zoo had other imperatives driving their decisions.

At the time one of the female vervet monkeys had given birth to a beautiful male baby and was doing her best to nurture and raise her bright-eyed son within the highly social vervet monkey group at the zoo. Unfortunately, as the young mother was at the bottom of the group's social hierarchy, both she and her baby were being attacked by other females within the group. This was because vervet monkey social structure is basically a matriarchy in which the more offspring a female has, the greater power and status she gains within the group. Also, because the enclosure area in which the group lived was a fraction of their natural territory size and the dominant female at the time was not breeding, she and some of the other females began to mercilessly attack the lower ranked female and her baby. Held captive within the vervet enclosure the young mother and son had little chance to escape this onslaught. Meanwhile the other Primate Keepers and I did what we could to keep the pair safe, but more intervention was required if we were going to save this pair from further harm.

Whilst working on a solution to provide protection for these two,

I was called to a meeting with zoo management. It was here I was informed that the decision had been made by the zoo's management to euthanise the baby monkey as the most effective way to address the issue. When I asked management how they had reached this choice, they explained that, "It was best for the animal." I couldn't comprehend how it would be best for either the baby monkey, who was going to be euthanised, or his mother, who was going to lose her baby. Worse still, I was told that I and others in the Primate Team were going to be involved in the process. This meant that we would have to physically remove the baby from his mother and take part in the euthanasia of this perfectly healthy being. To me, this did not make sense. It also went against every value that I believed zoos and their workers were supposed to uphold, especially when there was no real need to euthanise the baby. I felt the problem could have been solved by moving the existing group out from their confined existence into another more spacious enclosure.

Sadly, the zoo management directive won out over any attempts to change their decision. The baby vervet monkey was summarily taken from his mother and given a lethal injection by the zoo's resident vet. I found this incident extremely upsetting to witness and equally difficult to understand. I asked myself how an animal's life, one which we were meant to protect, could be so swiftly and cold heartedly extinguished. From this event and others like it, I came to understand that sometimes the zoo as an organisation, and the people in management positions, made many of their decisions with intellect alone. Here financial, logistical and business values were placed as of equal importance to those of animal welfare and conservation. Even though the zoo justified their actions by insisting that it was the best outcome for the animals, on this occasion they had made a purely financial decision, in its own best interests. Therefore, when they were assessing their responsibility in the matter, the money was valued over the greatest outcome for the animals concerned. As they could have saved the baby's life and spared its young mother the trauma of losing her first born in such circumstances.

This story illustrates that when the intellect is used alone, without the combined wisdom of the heart, it becomes a brutalising force instead of an informed one. Left unbalanced, decisions made and actions taken based solely upon the intellect can often be harsh, cruel and short-sighted. This is the issue we face as humans, where the cold hard nature of the intellect is prized above all else. This enables many decision makers to ignore alternative perspectives or facts that are contradictory to their preferred course of action. At the zoo it became the norm, in many cases, for management to consider that decisions such as the one regarding the baby vervet monkey were humane. Yet, the truth was that because of their business-based, intellect-centred values, they were instead the perpetrators of inhumane actions. This happens because humans have the ability to make choices and take actions even when we know they may be contradictory to some of our stated values and beliefs. Yet we proceed with these anyway and use our intellect to justify this stance.

Way of the Heart

'Educating the mind without educating the heart is
no education at all.'
Aristotle

On the other hand, when we *think* with the loving compassion of the heart we are open to understand and connect with all living beings. The hallmark of the heart is empathy, the ability to see another's perspective and feel an affinity with other life forms. The heart also enables us to care for and extend kindness to others. With the heart, we see ourselves as more alike than different, more unified than separate and more aligned than distanced. From this perspective, to be unwilling to assist another is akin to refusing to assist ourselves, because the wisdom of the heart has a unifying and selfless way of making sense of the world and our place within it. In addition, studies have shown that we make better choices when our heart is in a coherent and harmonious state, which is most likely to occur when we experience love, joy and inner peace.[91] With this in mind, to fail to embrace the native intelligence of our hearts does not make sense. Perhaps most importantly, without the heart engaged we cannot find happiness within ourselves, as happiness is love. So by cultivating the sense of love within us and then extending it to other beings, we come to see them as ourselves. This is where true love and happiness reside, at the point where we see no separation, and we see us in them.

As I have mentioned, the key here is to seek a balance between the heart and the head. To think and make choices solely based upon the emotion of the heart can lead also lead to poor choices. In some cases, it can lead to a type of hypocrisy, where we become enamoured with feeling good and being seen as special, rather than happily contributing without expectation of reward. Additionally, we can expose ourselves to the risk of blindly following the ever-changing array of erratic and impulsive drives, desires and attachments that arise when feelings alone govern our decision-making. This is because our emotional states can be random, volatile and arbitrary and need to be guided by the reason and logic of the intellect. Choices centred only on feelings and strong emotions, can end with disastrous results, such as crimes of passion, which can shatter lives forever. In another light, examples of heart-centred yet illogical choices can be observed in the following: When we say we love animals but have livestock animals killed for our culinary enjoyment, or when, in the form of indiscriminate charity, we give and act to feel good, yet the organisations we support may be undertaking ill-thought out programs causing more problems than they solve. Unfortunately I have witnessed the negative impacts of some such choices within this field, as the story below illustrates.

The Costs of Unintelligent Love

In the earlier story of the vervet monkey baby, I spoke about the dangers of using intellect alone for decision-making and to uphold organisational values. Conversely equally devastating issues are often created when we go to the other end of the spectrum, basing our choices and actions only on the emotions of the heart. This is especially true in the fields of conservation and animal welfare. I have experienced this first-hand where well-meaning yet, unintelligent actions can have damaging impacts upon the beings it is supposed to assist. This can be the case with some rescue and rehabilitation centres.

As previously explained, any baby orangutan found without its mother has most likely witnessed her slaughter at close range. This is because we know that no female orangutan will ever abandon her baby. In fact, she will defend her young one until her final breath. Usually the victims of poaching, the illegal pet trade and wholesale murder by loggers or developers during the clearing of their habitat for unsustainable forms of agriculture, baby orangutans are taken from their dead mother's arms. As aware and intelligent beings, these youngsters are traumatised by the ordeal of seeing their mother killed, being separated from her dead body, put into a cage alone, sometimes injured and often on-sold to local or international buyers in the illegal pet trade market. Understandably, by the time they are rescued and brought into rehabilitation centres they have experienced much suffering in their short lives.

Therefore, the aim of these centres is to repair the babies' physical and mental well-being as quickly as possible via nurturing and intensive care from experienced animal welfare staff. Once this is done, the next steps are to commence with their social and cultural training on 'how to be a functioning orangutan' and to teach them survival skills for possible release back into the jungle. This is an important but labour-intensive job and requires centres to fund these ongoing projects over many years.

Due to this, fundraising is an essential aspect of such programs.

In this case, whilst supporting a particular rehabilitation centre, we became aware of a program that offered volunteers the opportunity to become a 'mum' to an orphaned orangutan baby for a period of about six weeks. Which meant that the volunteer mums would be given a baby orangutan to care for over the entire length of the program. The process included daily, intensive contact with their assigned baby. Obviously the two would bond as a mother and baby do and these mums would shower love, affection and attention on these little orphans for this time. Unsurprisingly, this program was exceptionally popular in attracting well-meaning volunteers from Western countries to leave their homes and pay for the opportunity to share their love with a baby orangutan in need. These volunteers were good people, under the impression they were contributing to the survival of the Critically Endangered orangutans and helping out with the specialised care of the babies in a positive and proactive way. Because on the surface and to the uneducated eye, this seemed like a win-win, animal welfare-based act of charity with great outcomes for all involved. Using the compassion of their hearts, they joined the program without using their intellects to investigate the repercussions for the babies in their care.

However, once the six week program ended and the volunteer mums said good bye to their assigned baby orangutan, happily jetting back home, something disturbing occurred. In many cases, soon after the volunteer mothers had left, the baby orangutans ceased to thrive. They became listless, unresponsive and over a relatively short period of time, some even died. Despite this, the practice continued because the programs were so popular and attracted much needed funds for the work of the rehabilitation centre.

Still, the important question remained: why had these orangutan babies died? Did they contract a disease from their foreign carers? Was the level of the centre's care inadequate once the volunteer mums had left? Or, was it something else?

For me the cause was evident. The babies had died from the effects of a broken heart. Consider for a moment that the bond between an orangutan mother and her baby is known to be the strongest of all the Animal Kingdom. That these babies had already lost their mothers in distressing circumstances and arrived at the rehabilitation centres alone and traumatised. Then, suddenly, a new mother figure arrives, bonding with the infant and showering it with all the love, attention and affection the baby has missed from its own mother. This new mother does this every day for six weeks. It is easy to understand that the youngster finally feels it has found the mother and the love it has yearned for and would normally receive in the wild. To have this given, then taken away once more is simply too much to bear. This is why many babies died as a consequence.

At The Orangutan Project we have learned that unintelligent, compassionate love when applied in any field, including conservation, can be equally dangerous as the sometimes cold-hearted reasoning of the intellect alone. To be guided by either in isolation means that we are less able to appreciate the bigger picture, make informed choices and ultimately act for the greater good. This is why we work with both the head and the heart, both intellect and love to achieve the best outcomes for all beings involved.

It's all about creating a balance and a harmony between the two.

Therefore, in conservation, animal welfare and all areas of life, our task is to combine heartfelt empathy and love on the one side and then rationally apply the clarity of mind and reason on the other. In this way we can all begin to act intelligently and with compassion. When head and heart are aligned with love and compassion at the centre of our choices, we can grasp the greater purpose at play. In addition, we are no longer polarised or disturbed by the vagaries of emotion, so the mind is more peaceful and capable of seeing the whole solution not just the challenge in front of it. This is what I call the balance of the head and the heart, a state of being where we are able to see more clearly. With it comes balance of vision, a holistic way of seeing and thus bringing a greater meaning to life. Perhaps most importantly, we naturally move from being selfish and self-centred to being more selfless and life centred. This is a shift which we all need to make in our thinking.

Finding the Balance

On the eco tours we conduct to Sumatra and Borneo, I have the privilege to spend time and share insights with people from all over the world who choose to demonstrate and gain the benefits of this expanded way of thinking and being. We find that most of those who join us on these unique journeys experience them as life changing events. For example, prior to the tour, each participant commits to personally raising a set target of funds to contribute to the conservation work that The Orangutan Project supports in the field. This shows a dedication and commitment to the cause and the ability to engage in intelligent and compassionate charity. During the journey they are invited to visit some of the excellent conservation and animal welfare organisations with which we work. They also travel with us to the remote rainforests to see orangutans in their wild habitats. Some of these tours require treks and the willingness of participants to cope with tropical weather, native insects, local food, accommodation and facilities as well as being cut off from modern telecommunications from time to time. This means that the journey can take some outside their comfort zone. However, it is often because people are prepared to leave their daily lives behind and embrace the unknown that the greatest shifts are experienced.

The individuals on these tours are usually already our donors and supporters, so their love and respect for the orangutans we work to protect is obvious. Additionally, many of them are willing to travel many thousands of kilometres from their homes just to gain the experience of seeing orangutans in the wild. Yet they do so in the knowledge that they will not be able to touch, cuddle or hold the wild or rehabilitated orangutans which they encounter on the tour. This is because it is not in the best interests of the orangutans for them to do so. Human contact, without proper medical screening, can transmit diseases. Also, constant contact with humans can create dependency within the orangutans. This goes directly against our aim for the orangutans to live free and wild in their natural habitat. Importantly, those who take our tours agree to avoid physical contact with the orangutans, even though their emotional desires mean that they would absolutely love to be able to come into close proximity with our orange cousins. Therefore, the participants are able to practice respect, wisdom, compassionate and intelligent thinking by understanding what is best for the orangutans and by resisting their urge to be close to the beings they love. In this way they do the most good in the circumstances and come away from the experience as changed individuals.

It is easy to imagine the possibilities that would occur not only for us, but for all living beings, if each of us embraced and adopted this way of thinking. These are the gifts of thinking with a balance of the head and the heart.

In my own life, a second trip to India to spend time with my Guru would help me to further integrate my head with my heart.

A Second Invitation

The second invitation from Parthasarathy came a couple of years after the first, only this time the length of my stay in India was to be for two to three months. This was because he was conducting a lecture tour around the country and wanted me to accompany him on some of the journey. Additionally, my adventurous partner Wendy was to join me which would add a whole new dimension to the trip. The plan was that we would spend part of our time at the ashram and the other travelling with Parthasarathy on his lecture circuit. Furthermore, as my Guru wished for me to continue my learning process and deepen my experience, he had arranged for Wendy to be accommodated with wealthy friends of his whilst we travelled. However I was to discover that I would sometimes be living in a more simplistic, less lavish manner.

Stepping into the bustling crowds of Bombay airport I was once again reminded of the overwhelming nature of the city. As it was Wendy's first experience of India, she was naturally stepping out of her comfort zone and maintained a wide eyed amazement as she took in the sights and sounds of this seething metropolis. This time, with Wendy by my side, I made my way to Victoria Station once again and the long train ride into the Indian country side.

For the duration of this trip I was to live as a monk, dressed in simple robes and observe a humble life style. For example, in Bombay I lived with the other men from the ashram and slept on the top of a school in the slums of the city. As the school wasn't well looked after and the area was incredibly poor, when we walked out in the mornings there would be dead bodies lying on the streets. Yes, dead human bodies. This was because it was customary for people to put out the bodies of those who had died overnight onto the street and they would be dealt with during the day. We had to step over the bodies as we made our way out of the grounds in the morning. Shocking as it may sound to Western minds, this was the reality of life on the streets. The constant cycle of life and death was ever present. Yet this experience helped teach me that the opposite of death is not life, rather it is birth. As life is what happens beyond birth and before death and all is part of the reality of existence.

In the West we hide death away from sight and try to sanitise and separate it from our everyday lives. But by hiding death and attempting to mask our own mortality we lose the capacity to truly live, as we are ignorant of this part of the process and afraid of our inevitable passing with its unknown realm beyond. Life becomes unreal as we ignore what we all know to be the reality of death. However, if we accept death and embrace it, it would make the journey of life so much more precious and therefore wondrous to experience. This is because understanding that we will die helps us to appreciate life in all its beauty in the present moment.

Ultimately the paradox we experience in the West is that we choose to live a lie, collectively thinking we will live forever, yet knowing this is not true. Our ignorance around death and the cognitive dissonance which keeps this in place stops us from embracing the full measure of life. In the process we also lessen our ability to feel our own suffering and that of others so we can become monsters of our own making. As I travelled the Third Class train ride across the entire breath of India from Bombay to Madras, I was reminded of a line from John Milton's epic poem Paradise Lost, often quoted by my Guru. "The mind is its own place, and in itself, Can make a Heaven of Hell, a Hell of Heaven." [92] In that, external circumstances matter, however they are insignificant to the inner circumstances of our minds.

Back at the ashram with the Guru, Wendy and I spent our days in learning and contemplation as I had done on my first trip there. However, this time we were together and our relationship had developed to a new depth of love and understanding. It was during this time, that one day when I was standing at the communal kitchen sink washing dishes, dressed in the robes of a simple monk, that Wendy asked me to marry her. I said, "Yes." Things were moving forward in my life, on both the inner and outer levels. Importantly, as I became more comfortable with my inner world, my outer world reflected greater meaning and order.

As my time with the Guru at the ashram came to an end, I recall one of our last conversations as I wondered how I would integrate my new way of being into my everyday life back home. The Guru explained, whilst at the ashram I had been learning the philosophies and new information as an academic exercise. However, now it was *time to integrate this and bring it into practice. He went on to say that he could only be the signpost to point to me towards myself and my inner journey. The next step for me was to understand the direction I must follow and embrace this in all parts of my life.*

With this in mind, he told me that it was not helpful for students to continually come back to the ashram. He likened the process to a parent and a child, because if you have a child and the child has to stay with you always, you haven't succeeded as a parent or a family. A parent's job is to empower the child to go out into the world and create a life of their own. With a smile, the Guru then turned to me and said, "Leif, you have enough knowledge now to become self-realised. You don't need further knowledge and you don't need to come back. My work is done."

This was the last time that I would visit the ashram and my Guru in India. It was time for me to continue along my path alone.

Chapter Six
Convergent and
Divergent Thinking

'We are addicted to our thoughts.
We cannot change anything if we cannot change our thinking.'
Santosh Kalwar

Another Way of Throwing Starfish

Amongst philanthropic, conservation and animal welfare organisations the '*Throwing Starfish*' story is commonly used as a metaphor to illustrate the idea that we can each make a difference if we take action.[93] The difference may be small in the scheme of things, but it is a difference all the same. This is true whether it involves the rescue and care of a single living being or the protection of an entire species. If you haven't heard the story or need a quick refresher, the simple yet powerful tale goes something like this.

Early one morning, after a massive storm, a man is walking alone on a beach. As he walks he notices that tens of thousands of starfish have been washed up onto the shore, stretching as far as the eye can see. The tide is going out, so they are stranded on the sand, unable to return to their home beneath the waves. This means that the starfish are destined to perish as the morning progresses, either being dehydrated by the relentless summer sun or perhaps becoming a meal for a hungry predator. As the man continues his walk, he sees a young boy in the distance making his way towards him along the beach. The boy's journey is slowed because he regularly stops to reach down, pick up a starfish and throw it back into the ocean. As the man approaches the boy, he finds him reaching down once more to collect a starfish and throw it back into the sea. Stopping to speak with the child, the man asks him what he is doing. The boy answers that he is throwing the starfish back into the water so they don't have to die there on the sand. The man looks down at the boy and carefully explains, "There are tens of thousands of starfish on the beach. You know that you can't possibly make much of a difference in saving them. So why do you bother to throw a few back?" The boy slowly reaches down, picks up another starfish and casts it back into the sea. He then looks up at the man with a smile and says, "Well I made a difference to that one!"

As a call to action and an inspiring metaphor illuminating the idea that each life is important and that each action we take has an effect, the starfish story is a persuasive one. In fact, I have used this anecdote to illustrate the plight of the orangutans. In that, the child has undoubtedly made a difference to a good number of starfish. He is also taking direct action by following his simple solution to the mass starfish stranding. As such, some would say that there is nothing to fault in his approach, because at least he *is doing something* and is not deterred by the rational thinking of the adult male in the story. However, it's worth examining this story in terms of the bigger picture. As perhaps there are other ways we can think about conservation and solve the challenges we face in saving a species, protecting a habitat and making an effective difference at the individual level. [94]

Convergent and Divergent Thinking

*'Problems cannot be solved with the
same mindset that created them.'*
Albert Einstein

At school we are most often taught that there is a single correct answer to a question. The teacher teaches us the correct answer and during a test or exam we are asked to give this answer back to them. Thereby demonstrating that we have learned from the educational experience. Mathematics is a good example of this, whereby we are given a sum to calculate, an equation to solve or a formula to apply. Generally, the teacher is looking for the one correct answer to the maths problem. If we provide this answer and we receive the marks, however, if we come up with an alternative answer, we do not. Therefore, it is a simple right or wrong, correct or incorrect, single-focus process. In terms of conservation, this is called convergent thinking, a concept discussed by Malcolm Gladwell in his excellent book *"Outliers."*[95] Convergent thinking applies where there is one unequivocal solution or a single path to take to address the issues facing us, which we can identify using our intelligence and then apply in a linear fashion.

In our story the boy is exercising convergent thinking. He sees a problem and looks to solve it in one straightforward step. He sees starfish on the beach and thinks, *'I will throw them back and save some lives in the process.'* This is simple and intelligent. As previously mentioned, the boy's actions are contributing to the survival of the starfish he throws back and at least he is not standing by doing nothing at all. However, in addition to this way of thinking there is another, equally important approach to take because many of the challenges we face cannot be solved with just one easy solution. This is where divergent thinking is important as an additional way of viewing an issue. [96]

Divergent thinking is where imaginative, creative and multi-facetted thinking comes into play. When divergent thinking is involved, there is no one set solution, but instead there is a myriad of possible innovative and inventive choices we can make to gain the same or even greater results. Here I'll use human language as an example of this approach to thinking, as how we speak and communicate across the world can be achieved in a vast number of languages. As long as we express the message we are seeking to convey, is there truly one right or wrong answer? Furthermore, the creative and inventive minds of humanity have not only created thousands of unique verbal communication forms, but have also mastered body language, written languages, pictorial and symbolic versions, musical, digital, hand signing for the deaf and even emoji based versions of language. No doubt we will see new and innovative developments in the area of human language and communication in the future.

In the case of our starfish story perhaps there were some alternative ways for the boy to make a difference? Firstly he could have enrolled the man on the beach to begin throwing the starfish back into the water with him, doubling his results. He could have also gone back to his family, friends, school, local sporting club or community or put out a call on social media to enlist further support to create a concerted effort on the beach that morning. Once the teams of people were organised and throwing the starfish back to their marine home, he could have approached his state fisheries and wildlife agency to report the incident. He then could have asked whether this was a common event or if there were any causative factors that could be addressed. Maybe the starfish were suffering from a disease or were injured due to the effects of their beaching, and this would be an important piece of information to know. In addition to this, local marine biologists and conservationists could have been approached to discover if human activity was contributing to the problem. Alternatively, the boy could have sought out a specialised charity or animal welfare organisation that was already handling the situation to add his assistance to their cause. From here, he may have been able to start fund raising and attracting financial support to save and protect the starfish as a species.

On the other hand, if the boy was in Australia and the beach was along the eastern coastline parallel to the Great Barrier Reef, he may have discovered that these were indeed crown-of-thorns starfish. This invasive, prolific and destructive starfish species is destroying the Great Barrier Reef and causing major issues to this natural wonder of the world. In this case, he may have contacted the local council to remove all the starfish and have them dealt with in a more considered way. From this perspective, we can understand how and why divergent thinking is so key to the fields of conservation and animal welfare. Because, by their very nature, conservation and animal welfare deal directly with living beings, biological eco-systems, the environment and human activity as a diverse collection of interconnected elements. Additionally, each element has its own specific effects as well as requirements. Therefore, it's important we engage and apply the multidimensional methodology of divergent thinking to the issues at hand.

Importantly, I am not saying that either thinking approach is right or wrong, better or worse, because on occasion there is a straightforward, single answer to a problem. However, sometimes a simple answer just doesn't exist. Due to this, our choice must be to use both ways of thinking to solve the issues of conservation, animal welfare and the often complex world in which we live. Again, by employing the strengths of both convergent and divergent thinking we are always better-off and our results enhanced when there is a balance in the ways we perceive any situation. Also, by using these distinct thinking processes our outcomes are more robust and can move us towards sustainable long term solutions. So, I see it as both wise and compassionate to consider all possible options for navigating our way forward by combining the clarity of a single focus, with the diversity of paths a more creative approach provides.

Applying Convergent and Divergent Thinking to Orangutan Reintroduction

When it comes to orangutan rehabilitation and reintroduction programs there is a temptation to look for the magic bullet or single solution to solve an individual problem or address issues for the species as a whole. In this way, we tend to seek solutions that follow a set and forget approach. This is classically convergent thinking but we cannot just copy the starfish thrower and immediately return rescued orangutans back to the forest and expect them to survive. The simple fact is that orangutan rehabilitation and reintroduction does not always follow a straight forward path of action. This is because we are working with highly intelligent and aware beings. Beings who adapt and learn to live in their environment via a rich and in-depth culture passed on from mother to baby over many years of intense training and care. If this cultural instruction is disrupted, especially in the early formative years, there is much ground to recover before young orangutans will be ready to live free and wild in the forest once more.

In response to this, The Orangutan Project has taken a more holistic and multi-faceted view of the issues we face and used divergent as well as convergent thinking in our approach. I believe that rehabilitation and reintroduction programs should be based upon four inter-related building blocks. As with most building blocks, if we don't take care to ensure the strength and stability of each successive block the structure will be unstable and unsustainable and eventually the system will collapse. This is why we support a process which seeks to address the needs of each individual orangutan and provide a practical system based upon these key building blocks. We find this process is effective for the majority of orangutans we support within rescue, rehabilitation and reintroduction centres.

The four vital building blocks of orangutan reintroduction are as follows:

1. Physical Health
2. Mental Health
3. Social Health
4. Forest Skills

Physical Health

The physical health of a rescued orangutan is the first and most important concern for any rescue centre. Accordingly, if an orangutan is in poor health there is no point in doing anything else except attending to the orangutan's well-being and moving them towards recovery. Therefore, we need to prioritise the immediate physical health and medical needs above all else. For example, if the orangutan has been rescued in difficult circumstances, it may come into a centre with injuries, missing limbs, bullet wounds, or it may be mal-nourished or have a disease. In any of these cases, the physical health of the orangutan must be assessed and then addressed as soon as possible to give them the best chance of survival. When the rescued orangutan is a baby, we sometimes find that the baby has contracted a disease from close, ongoing contact with humans. These babies may also have lost fingers or limbs, or have cracked skulls or cuts across their faces due to the use of machetes in the slaughter of their mothers. These injuries occur as the babies would normally be holding on tightly to their mothers during the attack and are often wounded by the poachers or illegal pet traders in the process. Understandably these physical issues need to be taken care of urgently.

Unfortunately, in some instances with the babies, their injuries may be of a nature which is so severe that they will never be able to be returned to the wild. For example, they may be missing an entire limb or be blinded, which will greatly affect their ability to navigate life in their rain forest home. This is also the case if they have contracted diseases such as human hepatitis, because if they are reintroduced they may then pass on the infection to wild orangutans. This, in turn, could decimate wild orangutan populations. At present there is a number of orangutans who have contracted the human strain of hepatitis B and, therefore, require long term captive care for the rest of their lives. Obviously, this is not an ideal situation, so we must work to avoid spreading the disease any further amongst both captive and wild orangutans.

Once the physical condition of each rescued orangutan is determined, we can use different approaches to offer them the best standard of life possible into the future. This all depends upon their potential capacity to one day be released. For example, the orangutans who will recover their full health, can progress through the steps required for them to be released back into their natural rainforest habitat. This is, of course, the best outcome for them. On the other hand, for some of those orangutans who cannot be released, we support a number of excellent centres that are working to provide protected havens and dedicated island reserves where they can live out their lives in relative freedom and safety. In this way, at least there is some opportunity for them to live a good standard of life.

Mental Health

After the rescued orangutan's physical health is re-established, the next building block on their journey to well-being is their mental health. It is important to note here that this is an area that people often miss or neglect to address, however it is a critical part of the recovery process for our orange cousins. As it is easy to understand that if an orangutan is physically unhealthy, it is difficult for it to have good mental health as they are in pain. However, without a good state of mental health, rescued orangutans cannot go on to gain social health or learn the required forest skills. This means their mental health must also be addressed if they are to succeed in the next stage of their rehabilitation.

We have found that this vital step is often over looked because some veterinarians come from a purely physical perspective, considering animals somewhat like biological machines that simply have to be put back together to regain full health. Due to this, some vets may approach the care of orangutans a little like animal mechanics who can successfully repair the physical body but know little about them from a psychological perspective. Alternatively, perhaps they are more like biologists with a particularly scientific view point, so they see orangutans from the level of the species instead of the individual living being. So again, they do not realise the necessity of mental wellness for the individual orangutan.

To fully understand the plight of rescued orangutans it is key to recognise that they will likely arrive at the care facilities stressed, traumatised and under mental duress. In the case of mature wild orangutans, they will be unused to confinement or captivity and may have endured both physical and mental hardship prior to their rescue. Those who have spent most of their time in captivity in sub-standard zoos or as illegal prisoners as part of the exotic pet trade will generally have been caged and kept in stressful and abhorrent conditions. If held captive alone, orangutans will have essentially been kept in what amounts to solitary confinement.

On the other hand, they may have been subjected to unsuitable group enclosures, confined at close quarters with a number of possibly unrelated orangutans, which would be equally stressful. An appropriate analogy is that of human refugees who have been subjected to the challenging and stressful environment of a refugee camp. In such camps, there is little freedom, privacy or choice about with whom individuals share their space. Refugees also have little power to decide when they will leave or where they will live in the future. With this in mind, it is easy to comprehend the mental distress which occurs for captive orangutans and recognise that their mental health will have been compromised to some degree.

In the case of baby orangutans, it is vital to appreciate them as beings with the closest bond with their mothers across the entire Animal Kingdom. As mentioned earlier, orangutans live in semi solitary social structures and the mothers are the sole carers of their babies. This means that orangutan mothers don't appear to display the 'biological switch' to turn-off their bond with their young, likewise their babies are innately connected with their mothers. Therefore, losing their mother is a traumatic event for orangutan babies and they often suffer greatly when this close mother / child attachment is severed at an early age. Furthermore, this severance usually occurs in such a way that baby orangutans bear witness to their mother's death, possibly witnessing her being skinned and eaten by poachers. To then be taken away by the same individuals is obviously a huge ordeal, so their little minds are broken and in need of repair.

It is equally important to appreciate that, like humans, orangutans are intelligent, aware beings with complex mental capabilities and well developed memories. Due to this, the memories of these traumatic events can and do affect the young orangutans' psyches. This is why attending to their mental care is so essential. However, for rescued orangutans there is also a trade-off between time and care, because we have discovered that the smaller the orangutan is when it is released into the wild, the better chance it has for surviving in the natural environment over the long term. This is the case for a two key reasons.

1. If an orangutan is living in a cage or human environment during its crucial first years it will begin to adapt to life under these conditions and learn this way of living. Where instead, it should be adapting to life within a natural forest environment and amongst members of its own species. Therefore, long term confinement in a cage will encourage adaptation to this form of existence, and we don't want this to occur.

For example, sometimes when I visit the jungle forest training school and reintroduction site at BTP, I will see new orangutans arrive at the facility. They will be in holding cages and it is clear that some behave differently to others, depending upon how much time they have spent caged. Perhaps one acts strangely, sitting on the floor of the cage with its arms wrapped around itself, rocking back and forth in self-comforting behaviour. However, in the cage next door, another orangutan may seem relatively unperturbed.

When they are released from their cages, suddenly the situation is reversed: the strangely behaved one is immediately happy in its newly freed state, while the seemingly normal one is terrified of being out of the cage. What has happened is that the seemingly normal orangutan has adapted successfully to living in the cage and the other, wilder individual has not yet done so. The latter orangutan will do better in the forest. Therefore, what The Orangutan Project aims to do is to release them from their cages and into the forest as quickly as possible to avoid this adaptive response. At the same time, we attempt to strike a balance, providing them with as much care and preparation as possible before releasing them.

2. A smaller orangutan can quite easily find enough food to support its weight in the wild as it will not initially require much food to survive. A larger, more mature orangutan will require a greater amount of food to survive. The problem is that they may be equally poorly skilled and lacking experience in supporting themselves in their natural environment. Therefore, the bigger orangutan may starve to death because it cannot source enough food for its size. While the small one may survive as it has time to learn through culture and experience how to find enough food to support itself. The other side of the issue is that the younger orangutans require maternal love and care for their psychological wellbeing. In the wild, they naturally receive this from their mother, suckling until six to eight years old, sleeping with their mother and having her nurture, protection and care at all times. It is easy to appreciate the dilemma that we face in this regard. In many ways, we perform a balancing act between trying to release the orangutans back to the wild quickly so that they do not adapt to a human world and providing them with a sufficient basis of love, good mental health and culture.

Social Skills and Knowledge

Once their physical and mental health is stabilised, the next building block in the journey to freedom for these orangutans is the learning of social skills. At this stage, we place them with other orangutans so they are able to learn the appropriate social skills for life in the wild. These include interacting with other orangutans, learning communication skills and gaining a solid understanding of what it is to be an orangutan. This is an important stage because, much like humans, they learn from culture and from each other. Moreover, because they naturally live within a semi-solitary society, they need to learn how to interact with this society as they will encounter other orangutans when released into their natural habitat. This means they will need to understand and recognise the subtle and not-so-subtle signals and behaviours of others in the wild. In this stage they will also learn the importance of having friends and supporters to help with their social skills and these skills need to be developed via the socialisation process.

Additionally, what we have come to understand, especially with rehabilitated orangutans, is the vital importance of learning from culture. This is because these orangutans lose much of their culture when they lose their mothers since they are their major source of cultural and social instruction. Additionally, culture is the main way that orangutans adapt to their environment and, unfortunately, wild orangutans can't necessarily pass this on to them. However, the good news is that we have found that each rescued orangutan may have retained some part of their cultural knowledge and can then pass this on and teach others as they interact in the reintroduction centres. For example, one orangutan may be good at building nests, another may know how to source a type of food and another may display excellent climbing and tree navigation skills. Therefore, if these orangutans can socialise together and get along with each other, they can teach and learn from one another. In this way, they can combine their cultural knowledge which is far more effective than humans trying to teach each individual orangutan these kinds of skills.

In addition, we know orangutans are exceptionally clever, can invent things and can figure problems out for themselves. Thus, when they can learn together as a group, even if they have never done something previously, they can work it out and get on with it by themselves. Also, when a particularly smart orangutan solves problems or comes up with an innovative solution within a group, other orangutans can quickly learn from this example. In this way, they are learning from their learning and, therefore, multiplying its value within their social group. These examples demonstrate that this is a powerful and effective way to enable the social knowledge of these orphaned orangutans to be greatly expanded in a shorter period of time.

To underline the critical nature of learning social skills, it is valuable to consider how a human child who had not been exposed to normal family dynamics, social situations, peer playmates or regular human interaction would behave without these key elements of cultural and social learning. With this in mind, it is clear to see the immense value of gaining good social skills to equip us for life and to understand the costs involved when these formative influences are lacking. These same influences apply to orangutan social health and development.

Forest Skills

The last building block before release into the wild is the learning of forest skills, which provide orangutans with the knowledge to survive in the rainforest environment. This type of training includes how to make night nests. This skill is important for orangutans in Borneo but an absolute must for those in Sumatra, because Sumatran tigers are known predators of Sumatran orangutans. Therefore if an orangutan spent a night on the ground in the forest it could become tiger food before the night was over. As a result, it is imperative that they learn this skill for survival. Accordingly, when the youngsters are in jungle school at BTP, the technicians ensure that they are always taken back to the cage at night if they do not successfully make a nest to sleep in for the evening. The other vital elements for the orangutans to learn include recognising and sourcing a wide range of different foods within the forest, finding additional water in the canopy if needed, climbing and safely traversing their treetop home high above the ground.

Once the orangutans are reintroduced into a protected forest area, the technicians will generally follow and monitor them for at least three non-fruiting seasons. They do this to ensure the orangutans know a variety of non-fruit food sources and that they do know how to survive on their own. This means they are usually followed for an average of three years. To begin with, they are followed every day to confirm they know how to competently make a night nest and can identify and locate at least 120 different food sources, including key items such as rotan, figs and termites. These foods are important as they can be eaten during a non-fruiting season. (Interestingly, wild orangutans have a knowledge of around 2,000 to 3,000 different food sources; however we still do not know half of these and are trying to learn about them.) The key here is that we are aiming for orangutans to have mastered the basic forest skills during their rehabilitation to be able to survive in the wild.

When reintroduced orangutans have demonstrated the basic skills required for daily living, they are then monitored once a week. The telemetry teams are able to do this by locating the orangutans in the forest via small transmitters that we have had surgically implanted between their shoulder blades. Using the telemetry from the transmitter to find the orangutans as they move around their dense rain forest territory, the teams can check their level of health and confirm that they are managing to survive without assistance. With this system, we can also identify if the orangutans are not doing well or are ill and can then bring them back to the centre for care and retraining if necessary. If we find they may need more surveillance, we may return our checks back to the daily frequency to keep a closer eye on their progress. Unfortunately, on occasion, we may have to bring orangutans back to the centres because we discover that they simply cannot survive alone in the wild. This may be the case where the orangutans still aren't physically fit enough to be released for the long term. This can occur especially with larger animals who may have developed muscle atrophy whilst confined to a cage and so are simply not strong enough to carry their weight through the jungle canopy.

As you can appreciate, to progress a rescued orangutan through the four building blocks of preparation for release requires an intensive focus of time and effort. However, when we are successful in reinstating one of these magnificent beings safely in their natural home, it is a rewarding and valuable experience. Not only have we assisted an individual in need of support and care, we have also been able to play a part in ensuring the survival of the species as a whole. This is one of the aspects of the work we support that makes it all worthwhile. The story of one such journey for a young orangutan named Monti highlights some of the obstacles that we can overcome in the process.

Monti's Story

When it comes to stories of how we can approach orangutan conservation, Monti's journey is an excellent example of using both convergent and divergent thinking to help save individual orangutans and further the survival of the species. Especially when we work to create a safe and secure pathway for their long-term survival into the future. In this case we were able to support an excellent outcome for Monti and even assist in the care and rehabilitation of other orphaned orangutan babies in a unique and surprising way.

International Animal Rescue, (IAR) first heard of Monti's plight in 2009, when they were informed there was a very small baby orangutan being held illegally by a local family in a remote Bornean location. Once alerted, it took the rescue teams several days to reach and then rescue Monti. Timid and mal-nourished, this helpless orphan was held captive and most likely destined for the illegal pet trade and a lifetime of imprisonment. This was the case even though the family who held Monti assured rescuers that she had been found alone and destitute in the forest. However, knowing how female orangutans care for their young, rescuers understood that Monti's mother would never have abandoned her baby. Instead they could only assume that her mother was slaughtered in front of her terrified baby. Monti would then have been taken from her dead mother's arms and kept captive awaiting her sale into the cruel and unlawful exotic pet trade.

Still frail and traumatised by her ordeal, Monti immediately needed around-the-clock care by a specialist orangutan technician at the IAR Rescue Centre in Ketapang, West Kalimantan. Highly skilled and correctly trained in this task, the technician took care of Monti until she had recovered sufficiently and was physically strong and mentally stable enough to join other orphaned orangutans at the Orangutan Emergency Centre (OEC). Once there, she was able to commence her rehabilitation process. This included dedicated care, socialisation with other orangutans, the learning of culture and behavioural skills and an intensive jungle training school program. This program would teach her all the skills she would one day need to be ready for release into a safe forest habitat.

As part of The Orangutan Project's Orphan Adoption Program we were able to support Monti whilst she received excellent care at the rehabilitation facility. Over this time, we could also follow her development and receive reports and updates on how she was progressing. Monti excelled at forest school and she quickly learned to identify and source her own food, build nests and prepare for her new life in the jungle canopy. Under the careful supervision of the rehabilitation centre, Monti was finally ready for release to a secure island home at the wonderful IAR centre in West Kalimantan. Still under supervision and preparing for the time when she would be ready for release into the wild, it was here that Monti thrived.

However, this wasn't the end of Monti's remarkable story. During her time at the IAR facility is was noted that she was not only a very clever orangutan, but that she also naturally displayed friendly, motherly behaviour towards the other orphaned orangutans. Because of these characteristics, the team at the centre decided to involve Monti in a special trial surrogate mother program. This surrogate program was being piloted because mature female orangutans are known to exhibit the remarkable trait of naturally beginning to lactate when given a baby to care for, even if they have not given birth themselves. In this way, the concept was seen as a possible win-win for the older females who would have the opportunity to become surrogate mothers and for the orphaned baby orangutans who would benefit from nurturing maternal care. With the possibility of assisting both orangutans, Monti was given the chance to become a foster mother to a female baby orangutan named Anggun.

Little Anggun had been rescued when she was less than one year old and was still considered too young to be put in with the other orangutan orphans. Once she finished her time in quarantine at the centre, the team looked to find her an orangutan mother figure for comfort and security. So, the team introduced Monti and Anggun to each other and after a few days of socialisation, Monti and Anggun formed a close bond. Monti was able to teach Anggun new life skills including how to open a coconut, and she always allowed Anggun to drink and eat first. Interestingly, Monti seemed to have a natural talent when it came to motherhood, even discovering ways to calm Anggun when she cried as her maternal side came into play. Their bond was so close that the team often observed Anggun snuggled up on Monti's *belly when she was sleeping. Meaning that both baby and 'mum' were relaxed, comfortable and well bonded with each other.*

The story of Monti and Anggun is an encouraging example of how we can work with our donors' support and high-quality organisations to achieve excellent outcomes for individual orangutans and further support the survival of their three species. Not only was the surrogate program a rewarding learning experience for the individual beings involved, it also served to create a program which will be used into the future for helping other orphaned youngsters. For Anggun, it has been an important step forward in her rehabilitation, because she has found much needed comfort in Monti's caring arms and gained important cultural learning in the process. It has also been a valuable experience for Monti as she progresses on her way to fully mastering all of the skills she will need for adult life in the rainforest. We hope that one day this 'mother and daughter' pair will one day be released together to live wild and free. In this way, intelligent animal welfare and compassionate conservation initiatives can have significant positive impact on the orangutans it works to save and protect, creating a long-term win-win solutions for the future.

Section Three –
How we Act

'Vision without action is merely a dream.
Action without vision just passes the time.
Vision with action can change the world.'
Joel A. Barker

Ultimately, it is informed, compassionate action that brings all the stages of our journey together. As it is only by taking this type of solution-based, ongoing action that we can make the practical and lasting changes we seek to create for all living beings. Importantly, this action comes from the clarity of seeing through the veil of our biology and culture and from the wisdom and understanding that results from balanced thinking. We can now translate these two inner shifts of perception and thought into purposeful and effective action in the external world. However, this step is no longer about you or individual beings; rather, it is about all living beings collectively on the planet. As we are each part of the web of life and what we do to other species we ultimately do to ourselves. Therefore, by expanding our way of being in the world, we can focus on conserving, protecting and valuing all life forms and the planet we call home. To do this we need to unify our focus and collectivise with others to provide the greatest opportunity to effect positive change, because when we work together with co-operation and collaboration, we can truly change the world for the better.

Chapter Seven
It's Not About You

'Cherish the natural world because you are part of it
and you depend on it.'
Sir David Attenborough

Anthropocentrism and Biocentrism

Within the fields of environmental ethics, there are two key concepts that I feel best demonstrate the most significant shift that we, as humans, can make as a foundation for all our actions. One places humans in the centre of its focus and the other places us alongside all other living beings. As straightforward as this difference sounds, these two frameworks for considering our place in nature are worlds apart. Yet, if we can understand why the first is unsustainable and embrace the latter as a way of moving forward it could make all the difference for our collective futures.

Anthropocentrism – This is the school of thought that posits human beings, and their associated interests, as the central - and therefore the most important - on the planet. From an anthropocentric viewpoint the value of other beings or non-animate objects, rests in their capacity to benefit humans. Necessarily, human beings and our perspectives are deemed of the highest significance and some opponents liken this perspective to a form of human supremacy.[97] In many ways, anthropocentric philosophical arguments are closely aligned with most Western religions and their culturally embedded approach to the natural world. [98] This way of perceiving humankind's position as superior to that of other living beings is also recognised as one of the key contributing factors to the environmental issues we now face on the planet.

Biocentrism – This is a philosophy that recognises the intrinsic worth and, therefore, the value of every living being. Here each life form has the moral right to be treated with respect and viewed as an inter-related component of the web of life. From the perspective of biocentrism, the relationship between human beings and the rest of the living world needs to be re-explored, re-considered and most importantly, re-addressed.[99] As from this standpoint, humans are simply one amongst all other species and, therefore, other living beings do not exist to serve our needs and wants. It follows that biocentrism embraces the concept of extending compassion to all living beings.[100] The work of Albert Schweitzer, noted theologian and physician, echoed this sentiment with his philosophy of maintaining a, *'reverence for all life.'* [101]

There are four fundamental tenets that underpin biocentrism and these highlight the inherent worth and interdependence of all living beings. These are:

1. *"Humans and all other species are members of Earth's community.*
2. *All species are part of a system of interdependence.*
3. *All living organisms pursue their own "good" in their own ways.*
4. *Human beings are not inherently superior to other living things."* [102]

This means that ultimately, if we can extend our humanity from ourselves to all other living beings, we can only arrive at the following conclusion: It's not about you.

It's Not About You, It's About Us

This may seem like a direct contradiction to the ideas discussed in Chapter Four where the focus was '*All About You.*' However, the inner journey is a step we each must take to realise that the reverse is true. This comes with an expanded awareness and the understanding that we are all connected as living beings. Thus, the actions we take for the future shift from being all about ourselves as individuals, to focusing on the higher good of all- that is, of us. As part of this shift, we immediately drop the false separation of seeing ourselves within a 'them and us' paradigm. This frees us to see the oneness of all life. Besides, if we observed our planet from the perspective of outer space, we would see that every life form on the planet, including humans, are Earthlings; we all call this place our home. Therefore, every action we take is not about you, it is about all of us, about every living being.

Selflessness

The great news is once we embrace this way of perceiving and acting in the world, a number of seemingly paradoxical outcomes begin to flow into our life. This is called the selfless paradox, where by letting go of our usual self-centred existence, we receive everything without pursuing it. Also, once we stop pursuing happiness and choose to work for the benefit of all, to serve others and make the world a better place, we become happier. This means that we become able to do truly good work that has greater efficacy and, as a result, we experience more love, joy and peace of mind. Interestingly, truly good individuals don't know that they are good, because they have become selfless and no longer pursue the things of the outside world for themselves, nor do they seek recognition and external reward for their work. Instead, they naturally express the joy within, and their actions correspondingly take on a greater order and effect in the world. Yet, we cannot fake this state of being, or pretend to be selfless whilst harbouring inner attachments to name, fame, power and money. Instead, to reach this state, we must become aware of human selfishness and then go beyond it.

There is another key aspect of the selfless person that is important to clarify. They never sacrifice anything whilst doing good. Sacrifice is a word that implies there is a cost to being altruistic; however, the reverse is true. For example, I am often asked how I gave up meat to become a vegan. I simply answer that I did not give up meat because I do not desire it. Instead, I simply transitioned to a way of eating that was more meaningful to me and left meat and animal products behind. So the truth is that I did not sacrifice anything. Much like an adult who has out grown the toys of their childhood, it is no sacrifice to leave these toys behind and go onto other pursuits. This is because, they no longer hold value for you or relevance and therefore, you leave them behind and move forward.

Something that I have observed in my own life, is that the more I was able to let go of my ego and self-centred-ness, the better I felt. This was true for me, physically, mentally and at a deeper level within myself. At the same time, I also became more aligned with my purpose to serve and make a difference for orangutans and other living beings. As this process took place, I found increased energy reserves and a greater fulfilment in my life and work. Therefore, it is often the case that a truly good person is full of energy, happiness and joy, and experiences boundless energy, power and efficacy in their endeavours. Ultimately, the selfless individual is more productive, to the extent that people look at them and ask, 'How?' Others consider that a life lived this way is full of sacrifice; however, becoming selfless is full of joy, happiness and inner peace. The truth is that the selfless individual does not miss out on anything and is able to undertake good work and live a worthwhile and fulfilling life. This is the truth of selflessness.

Selfishness

On the flip side of this, if we haven't reformed ourselves within and seek money, fame, name and power in the external world, there is a trap. The trap is that of the ego, by which some are attached to the idea of 'being good' and 'being seen to be good.' This puts them at odds with others, because outwardly they present themselves as selfless, yet internally they are selfish and still desire to obtain what they want. For example, this can sometimes be observed in the conservation community, where individuals work in a seemingly selfless way, yet they also carry ulterior motives. This is where sacrifice appears, as they are doing their conservation work for the purpose of ego, not the greater good. Internally, they want to feel that they are good people, and perhaps better than others, and justify this to themselves because they are sacrificing for the cause. Yet, all the while they want something out of their work such as reputation, power, wealth and fame.

This type of sacrifice is exhausting, instead of being inspired and energised by the process, these individuals are worn out by it and constantly require holidays to refresh themselves and regain their energy. Here lie the seeds of destruction for the work they do and the organisations they create, as the cycle of sacrifice and lack of energy is unsustainable. This is why everything that selfish people do in the external world is transient and eventually falls apart. When this occurs, they tend to blame others for their lack of success, as they are not consciously aware of the underlying issues. As a consequence of this they fail to see that they are caught in a trap of their own making. Unfortunately, from this position there is no way of rectifying the situation, unless they go within. They will resist this or will not even be able to consider the concept. Instead, as they are likely to be suffering internally, they will go for the short-term solution to relieve their pain. Such a solution can involve alcohol, drugs, addictions or distractions. Selfish people will take anything to avoid pain, grabbing at what is available as they need relief simply to feel good in the short-term. They can attempt to rationalise these actions because they wish to avoid their suffering, yet this is ultimately unsustainable. This is the truth of selfishness.

It's important to briefly cover what I mean by doing good and being good in the true sense of the word.

Exercising True Humanity

> 'When I do good, I feel good. When I do bad, I feel bad. That's my religion.'
> Abraham Lincoln

Firstly, the concept of *being good* and *doing good* is where we begin to act in a manner which is designed to benefit others. In fact, the drive behind *doing good* is to assist others, rather than the typical self-interested motivations which are focused on benefitting ourselves. Closely aligned with the paradox of selflessness, *doing and being good* is actually of great benefit to the individual who does the *good*. This means that by giving and being of service to others, we also gain as a result, yet we are not, and cannot be, motivated by any return to ourselves. This is evidenced in the scientific studies which have outlined a number of specific physical, mental and emotional benefits experienced by those individuals who not only do *good*, practice being *good* but who are intrinsically *good*. [103] These include enhanced mental and physical health, longevity and an inner sense of well-being. [104]

This is not a new nor ground breaking idea, but is one which has foundations amongst all of the great philosophical belief systems in the world. To understand this principle is to grasp the idea that it is in our own, as well as our collective interests, to *do good* for others.

Quite simply, it appears that we do better when we help others to do the same. Therefore, when we practice this principle as individuals, we widen our circle of focus to embrace the well-being and happiness of others, instead of focusing solely on our own needs, wants and desires. Some may call this altruism, others view it as following the law of reciprocity whilst others may see this as a form of flower-power liberalism. However, no matter what the label, many across the globe are beginning to wake up to the key benefits this way of thinking offers to all of us.

In fact, some have not only identified what *being good* means, they have also begun to measure it amongst the countries of the world. This is reflected in the landmark work of Simon Anholt and The Good Country Index.[105] In this index, each year the nations of the world are ranked according to the relative amount of good they do in the world. Based on seven specific categories of measurement, those countries which are recognised for doing the highest amount of good, are also amongst the most prosperous in the world.[106] As Simon Anholt states in his TED Talk, "*Which Country Does the Most Good in the World?*", "*To do well, a country must do good.*" Furthermore, this measure of "*good*" is not based on being morally good, but rather on how much the country does for other nations and people around the world. Anholt explains that the Good Country Index looks for how much a country contributes to making the world, "*...safer, better, richer and more caring.*" Interestingly, it appears that in return, other nations prefer to deal with "good" countries, so we see the benefits that being and doing good provides. [107]

I think it is key to remember that each country is made up of individuals who also subscribe to the idea that the more good we can do, the better it is for all of us. Therefore, without doubt, our small daily actions and behaviours can each contribute to the greater good of all. This is an empowering idea to understand and an even more inspiring stance with which to move forward in our lives.

For me there came a time where I saw the need to take proactive steps in the outer world.

Acting on Behalf of Others

Once I had said farewell to my Guru in India, life seemed to move quickly as my inward focus began to turn outward. Firstly, I founded The Orangutan Project in 1998 to ensure the survival of my friends the orangutans. I was no longer prepared to sit back and silently witness the wholesale destruction of their habitat nor the cruel mistreatment and needless slaughter of these remarkable beings. With this in mind, I had also finally come to a number of inescapable conclusions:

1. *All orangutans, no matter their circumstances, deserved Compassion, Protection and Freedom.*
2. *That alone, I could make a difference, but only a small one at best. However with a committed, focused team, a co-ordinated organisation and a group of like-minded supporters along-side us, we could make a large scale impact on an ongoing basis.*
3. *There was no time to waste and the orangutans needed our help and assistance sooner, rather than later. It was time to act as a focused organisation.*

Therefore, starting with a small committed group of individuals, we formed the original team at The Orangutan Project. The organisation has been consistently working towards improving the welfare and ensuring the survival of all orangutans ever since. With the success of our work for orangutans, I went on to found the International Tiger Project, the International Elephant Project and Wildlife Asia as proactive and collaborative conservation and animal welfare organisations. I had witnessed that when we worked together with others we could make an ongoing difference in saving many Critically Endangered species and their habitats.

On the personal front, a year later Wendy and I were married in an intimate ceremony in Las Vegas and we continued our lives together as a husband and wife team. My inner journey also continued as a daily, and often moment by moment process of self-discovery, gently tempered by the wisdom that Parthasarathy had passed onto me. As my Guru had explained the importance of reforming the mind through a practice of constant awareness, or as some call it, 'mindfulness.' Much like a spiritual practice, this was not a part time occupation, instead it is a full time way of being. This meant that it was always part of my consciousness as I was fixed on my deepest identity and truth, whilst still participating in life.

Ultimately, I left the zoo and stepped more fully into my role within the fields of conservation and animal welfare. Along this journey my work also became to support vulnerable local communities within the regions within which we worked for wildlife. I was also able to travel more widely and meet and mix with many other like-minded individuals across the planet. In this way, I was able to combine my love for conservation with a broader perspective and appreciation for true humanity whereby we each work together for the greater good of all living beings. It has been a personally rewarding and fulfilling path to share this with others along the way.

However, it is always a learning process as we seek to find the best solutions for all in the field.

Fallen Ranger

In the arenas of environmental conservation and animal protection, the work in the field can often prove to be both demanding and dangerous. Mindful of this, at The Orangutan Project, we are always prepared to act with both the clarity of our vision and compassion for others. When the lives of individuals with whom we work are on the line our thoughts and actions need to be balanced and focused upon the best result for all. Every life is important and our perceived interests should not be the determining factors when saving a life, especially when we have the means and ability to do so. This was certainly the case when I received an urgent call late one evening from one of the great organisations we support, which operates Wildlife Protection Units in Indonesia.

As I listened to the concerned voice of my colleague on the other end of the phone, my mind raced to understand what type of urgent event could have happened to cause a call at this late hour of the evening. He quickly explained that one of their rangers had gone missing in torrential rain whilst on patrol near a fast-flowing river. It appeared that he had fallen into the water and was swept downstream along the swollen waterway. Although the team had been searching for him for some hours, he was nowhere to be seen. Therefore, he was contacting me to ask permission for money to cover the cost of a search and rescue helicopter to look for the ranger before it was too late. Without a moment of hesitation, I responded that they should immediately arrange the helicopter and go out to find him as there was no time to waste. They needed to look for him now to have a chance to save his life. More importantly, I wanted to stress that it was 'not about the money' in urgent life and death situations such as these, the life of the ranger was more important. What mattered was to act straight away. Wishing them good luck in the search, I guaranteed the funds and told him we would talk about details later, once the ranger was found.

We spent a difficult couple of days waiting for news of the ranger's rescue. However, tragically his lifeless body was found floating in the river and it was clear that he had succumbed to the fast currents and drowned. We were deeply saddened at the loss of this experienced and dedicated ranger and sent word that we would like to assist his widow and children in the aftermath of this tragedy. Soon after this, I received another call from the team seeking approval for the funds to help the ranger's widow and young family. One of their major concerns was how they were to handle the acknowledgement of who gave the money to the ranger's family. My response was that they were to simply give these to the widow in person and ensure that she received the necessary funds. At a time such as this, the important thing to do was to take care of our people without concern for recognition, as it simply didn't matter. After all, a good young man had died whilst protecting orangutans and their habitat, and his family had lost a much-loved husband, father and son. Furthermore, if this situation was to ever happen again, I instructed the team to, "Just get in the helicopter and go. Let me know about it later as we would find the money somehow."

I discuss this particular example to illustrate that sometimes, ensuring that a donor first agrees to the redirection of their donated funds or is assured of being specifically recognised can slow down our work. Furthermore, it can interfere with effectively helping those who need our assistance quickly. In defence of my colleague's action in calling me to receive the go-ahead for the search mission for the ranger, I have learned that sometimes such action is necessary. From experience, some funding organisations are more concerned about being in control and gaining recognition than about the lives and welfare of other living beings. Therefore, my colleague was wary of acting without permission and was in many ways following necessary procedures.

Taking Right Action by Collectivising

I am often approached by concerned and compassionate individuals after my talks and presentations around the world. Invariably, they wish to know how and where they can best support our efforts to save and protect native habitats and the living beings who live within these environments. Apart from recommending that they start donating or volunteering with the cause straight away, as of course this will help, I generally also suggest that they educate themselves about orangutans, the work we do and the organisations we support with their funds. This is because I believe in informed action over the long term. This means that before we jump into action and begin trying to help, it is wise to understand the best course to take. This translates to grasping how to collectivise and work together with compassion and respect to achieve the greatest possible outcomes for those we seek to protect.

For example, sometimes people have taken up the 'think locally and act globally' mantle and begin to do what they can at the personal level to support the environment or their favourite cause. This can mean that they choose to go vegan or vegetarian, grow their own vegetables, use solar power and renewable resources, recycle and go palm oil free and so on. All of these actions are fantastic and, they do make a difference, but they alone are not going to change the world. However, if we combine our personal efforts and initiatives with collectivising through organisations in the field and work together, we can make a difference at the global level. As we can solve problems as a group, so our choices need to contribute to both the local and global arenas for the maximum benefit. In this way, we can reach towards the wider-interest of being globally good.

Additionally, it is important that we authentically care for others. This care also must also extend beyond the boundaries of our family, friends, loved ones and local communities, especially if we wish our actions to have a long-term, sustainable effect on the wider environment. If our compassion does not encompass all of us, we will be unable to effectively act for others. Again, this requires another expansion of our outlook and the scope of our work. Some good-hearted, compassionate individuals find this difficult because they are so attached and identified with their immediate family and friends. However, expanding our scope of care does not mean that we care any less for our loved ones; instead, we are extending the horizon of our care to include more compassion and love. In this way, we expand as individuals by bringing the care and desire for the well-being and happiness of others into our conscious awareness.

My Guru often said, "*Whatever starts off sweet ends up bitter, and whatever starts off bitter ends up sweet.*" Therefore, if your mind is telling you that the journey involved in becoming a good person is too hard, please understand that it is the way of life. For example, as a young person, you could choose to spend your time partying and having a good time or studying for a career. One is certainty more enjoyable in the beginning, however, in the end, the other choice, at first perhaps more bitter, will bring more joy and long-term success. The path that may be initially the most difficult will ultimately lead to the greatest outcome in life. This is the wisdom of starting that which is challenging. Life becomes happier and more peaceful when we understand this universal rule

As discussed in Section Two, thinking with the balance of heart and head is essential to taking the right action. This involves the two wings of the bird working together to create a wise, holistic approach to conservation. On the other hand, if we act indiscriminately, with well-meaning but uninformed conservation, it can have devastating negative effects. In some cases, such actions can go as far as to worsen the situation for the living beings and environments that they aim to assist. Indiscriminate charity is usually carried out by good people with good hearts who have not thought clearly about an issue, so even though they act with good intentions, their efforts do not produce the results they wish to achieve. Because of this, valuable time, effort and funds can be wasted, and the outcomes can cause more problems than they solve. This is why how we see, think and act must be balanced in order to effect positive change in the world. In this way, we all benefit.

Conservation and Animal Welfare

The terms *conservation* and *animal welfare* are often used interchangeably by those outside these fields. However, for many within these arenas, there is a distinct difference in the meaning and practical application of each. For example, in the case of wildlife conservation, the main focus is the survival of a species as a whole and not necessarily that of individual animals. Whereas those who are animal welfare advocates place great value on each individual life. That is, all animals matter and it is considered worthwhile to save each one. For example, an individual practicing animal welfare may raise money to rescue one orangutan from the illegal pet trade or cruel captivity. In this instance, the conservationist may say that this is a waste of time and money, as the life of the one individual is less important than the survival of the entire species.

Furthermore, the conservationist may put forward the rationale that the perspective of animal welfare embodies a lesser understanding than the broader perspective of the conservation of a species. They may conclude that any work should always be concerned with saving the species and not the individual animal. From this point of view, some individuals are expendable. However, I question this stance. Why can't we use the balance of the head with the heart, combining reason with creativity in our thinking so that we can act to save individuals as well as the species? For me, these two outcomes are not mutually exclusive. I have realised that there is always a way if we see clearly, think in a balanced way and apply purposeful action in each situation.

At The Orangutan Project and many other wildlife protection organisations we support, we use a two-pronged approach to achieve the best results for both the welfare of individual animals and the survival of specific species. These are based on the following principles:

Firstly, the best welfare outcome for wildlife is to be free and safe in the wild. Secondly, the best overall welfare outcome per dollar of funds donated by our supporters is in protecting wild populations and working towards the survival of the species. Therefore, when we save individuals and then highlight their plight it helps raise support, because people recognise that the individual matters. From this support, we can fund the protection and reestablishment of wild populations in protected ecosystems.

As such, both aims are achieved as they function hand in hand. At The Orangutan Project this is what we do in all the operational structures we create and use in our work. As we consider every orangutan is of equal value, whilst also aiming to direct the greatest amount of money to where it helps the largest number of individuals. However, we still need to help the individuals. In this way, our actions are of benefit to all living beings and demonstrates true humanity. We are all conscious beings and we each deserve the best possible outcome in every circumstance. This applies whether we are working for a human or non-human being, as we each have the right to live free and to be accorded respect for our individual lives, as illustrated in the following story.

Intelligent Animal Welfare and Compassionate Conservation

For an aware, sentient being such as an orangutan, being held in captivity in a zoo environment is generally not a positive experience. Still, as I discussed in my last book, at least some modern zoos have gone to great lengths to provide the orangutans in their care with the best facilities possible to maintain their mental and physical well-being. Unfortunately, this remains the exception rather than the norm and some zoos around the world still hold their captive orangutans in appalling conditions. This was the case for Sam, a mature female Sumatran orangutan who was living in dreadful circumstances in a Malaysian zoo. However, I am happy to say that Sam's story is a demonstration of how a group of committed individuals can make a life-changing and ongoing difference in the lives of our captive orangutan cousins and their offspring.

We first encountered Sam after she was rescued from a Malaysian zoo and taken for initial care at the Sumatran Orangutan Conservation Program (SOCP) Orangutan Quarantine Centre in North Sumatra. She was soon transferred to the BTP rehabilitation and release program in Jambi, Sumatra. As Sam was a mature female who had spent much of her life in captivity, surrounded by the bars of the zoo's enclosure instead of her rainforest home, we did not have much hope that she would ever be able to survive again in the wild. She was culturally unaccustomed to life free from captivity, in that, she had little to no knowledge of food sources, seasonal fruiting, nest building and other skills required for life in the forest. Also, due to her poor treatment in captivity, her physical and mental condition was poor. She was more used to the lonely, sad existence she had experienced hanging on the bars and ropes of her cage than to navigating the lush trees and vines of the forest canopy. Hence, the general consensus was that Sam would probably never be released into the jungle and, if this was attempted, it would take years of training for her to become competent enough for permanent release.

However, the team at the rehabilitation centre was determined to return Sam to physical and mental health and began to work with her. With The Orangutan Project supporting the organisation with their excellent rehabilitation work, there was a steady and marked improvement in Sam's well-being. During her stay, Sam was housed at night in one of the large and spacious training enclosure cages. Unbeknownst to staff at the centre, Sam had been able to attract the attention of a re-released male by the name of Rocky. Being an intelligent, determined red-blooded male, Rocky had discovered a way to mate with Sam, an equally red-blooded mature female, through the bars of her enclosure. I am sure you can imagine the result of this tryst between Sam and Rocky. Soon the staff were both excited, and somewhat concerned to learn that Sam was pregnant.

With this news we were now faced with a dilemma. We didn't want Sam's baby to have to live in a cage all its life because Sam could not be safely released. Plus, if we did not devise a solution quickly, the new baby would learn to live this way instead of adapting to the wild. We were faced with the prospect of having not only one orangutan who couldn't return to the wild, but two. This was not an ideal situation. We had to find a way to help them transition into the wild together. It was a unique challenge and one for which we would urgently need to raise funds – not just to ensure their successful joint release, but also to provide intensive monitoring and follow up. However, in the meantime Sam's adventurous baby boy, Cupcake, was born. From that point onward Sam and her cheeky ginger haired baby were inseparable.

To address the situation, we created a special appeal through The Orangutan Project's adoption program designed to train and support both Sam and Cupcake to be released into the wild under supervision. This meant that once Sam was trained in the key areas of rainforest life, she and Cupcake could be introduced into the wild with ongoing support and monitoring. Thus, Cupcake could at least grow up in his jungle home and learn how to be a free and wild orangutan. The good news is that Sam and Cupcake have been successfully released into a protected area of rainforest and are doing well. Better still, Cupcake is learning to live in his natural habitat.

Naturally wild orangutans are interacting with the pair and Cupcake is able to play with other baby orangutans, learning from them in the process. Therefore, even though it may not be possible for Sam to be fully independent the reintroduction program will be successful on a generational basis. Cupcake will live free and his future offspring will become fully wild. Even though Sam may not be able to be completely independent, she is in the best situation that she can be as she lives free from captivity. Additionally, our commitment to Sam is that The

Orangutan Project will support her life in the forest forever, so she is living in the rainforest and is regularly monitored. If she doesn't find enough forest food then she is fed by the technicians who support her. While all of our released orangutans receive careful motoring to ensure their health and safety, this little pair are extra special - and vulnerable.

The story of Sam and Cupcake is a one that inspires hope for the future, both for once captive and re-reintroduced orangutans. It also reinforces our commitment to continue working through the difficult challenges that can occur in animal welfare and conservation. It is encouraging that this once sad, lonely orangutan- who was forced into a captive life designed for human entertainment- is now a healthy, happy mother to a gorgeous youngster. Now Sam and Cupcake are living free and are contributing to the survival of their species as two individuals who can each produce offspring due to their exposure to wild fellow orangutans. This is all because of the concerted efforts of wonderful organisations on the ground in Indonesia, our ongoing donors and the co-ordination of the team at The Orangutan Project. It appears that with the right approach, love and life always find a way.

Chapter Eight
Balancing the Masculine
and the Feminine

'But humankind is masculine and feminine,
not just man or woman.'
Carl Jung

As the yin and yang symbol from Eastern traditions illustrates, humans possess both masculine and feminine aspects within our psyches. These aspects also express themselves in the outside world through our actions and behaviours. However, it is clear that the masculine and feminine are currently out of balance across the planet, in that, we have placed more emphasis and value upon the *yang or masculine* aspect of our nature at the expense of the *yin or feminine*. In doing so, we have created an imbalanced perspective within humanity. Therefore, we must re-balance the masculine and the feminine by empowering women and reinstating the feminine principle to its natural position alongside the masculine within society. This one step alone would create a shift in the way we approach conservation, the environment and the survival of all living beings, including ourselves.

Importantly, when I speak of the masculine and feminine, I am not referring specifically to the male and female genders. Instead I speak of what Carl Jung, defined as the masculine and feminine archetypes of the *anima and animus*. The anima refers to the unconscious feminine aspect within the man, and animus the unconscious masculine aspect within the woman. However, men and women contain both the masculine and feminine to some degree.[108] Jung considered both masculinity and femininity of equal worth and value, as 'two halves of a whole, such as light and shadow, halves which ought to serve to balance one another out.'[109]

The key characteristics of each archetype are identified as follows.

Masculine - The masculine is the active, aggressive, animating force, providing defence and achieving short term goals. It is characterised by logic, reason, action, firmness, survival, loyalty, rationality, adventurousness and strength. This aspect is represented by civilisation, production, order and the mind.[110]

Feminine – The feminine is the nurturing, caring, receptive force. It bonds within groups, is co-operative and cohesive and embodies sustainability and long-term balance. It is characterised by intuition, nurture, expressiveness, healing, gentleness, wisdom, patience, emotionality and flexibility. This aspect is represented by nature, distribution, chaos, and the heart.[111]

How were these roles defined in our hunter-gatherer past?

Our Tribal Hunter-Gatherer Past

Humans are social great apes. Accordingly, for the majority of our history, humans have lived a rich and highly adapted hunter-gatherer existence. As communal beings, we would gather into tribes of up to around 150 people. Interestingly, this is approximately the largest number of individuals with whom we can effectively associate and relate with in a social group and still maintain cohesion.[112] These tribes were generally nomadic and based around the willingness of tribe members to follow a leader and abide by the accepted social norms and cultural structures. Our very survival depended upon being a part of the tribe, fitting in, belonging to the group and believing in the same ideas. This was, and still is, a powerful evolutionary factor that helps to ensure the survival of both the tribe and the individual. Even to the extent that to this day, humans demonstrate this factor as we will often choose to believe some of the most unusual concepts, theories, myths and culturally driven ideas simply to remain a member of our chosen tribe. This often means ignoring scientific fact and common sense, in order to belong and avoid being excluded from the tribe. Examples of this behaviour in modern times include religious cults, extremist groups and fanatical political parties to name a few.

It is recognised that, based upon physical strength and biological features within the hunter-gatherer tribe, there were traditional divisions of labour. That is, men were most likely to go out in groups as hunting parties to source wild prey for food or defend territory and the women would form into gathering groups to collect, prepare and cook locally available fruits, berries, grains, herbs and wild produce. The women also had the task of caring for and looking after infants and young children, and these were best kept away from potentially dangerous hunting parties and the prey they sought. According to these divisions, the males acted as the prime protectors and the providers of high value food and the women took the role of preparing and distributing the produce to members of the tribe so everyone received their share. Therefore, each tribe member contributed to the survival and wellbeing of the tribe, with both roles being seen as of equal importance

As part of a nomadic tribe, individuals also had little personal property because whatever was owned personally needed to be carried on the constant journeys to new areas in nearby territories. Nomadic life also meant that there was no 'land ownership' in the sense that we understand this concept in today's terms. Due to this, hunter-gatherer tribes tended to maintain communal property, meaning that there was little need to control and restrict female or male sexuality and mating preferences. Under this tribal order, a female could exercise her choice in mate selection and pair-bond with a preferred male. However, she could also follow her instincts to mate with other higher value males when she was in oestrus and, thus, fertile. This is another adaptive behaviour for survival which still holds true to this day because, if modern heterosexual women are shown pictures of men when they are not in oestrus, they will generally select a nice sensitive type of male who will be kind and caring enough to help them raise their children. However, when most of these same women are in oestrus, and are shown the same set of photos, they will usually choose the strong, macho type, because they are looking to mate and create biologically strong offspring. [113]

For an example of how a tribe might operate in this way, consider a male warrior (Warrior 1) who leads a nomadic hunter-gatherer lifestyle. In this scenario. Warrior 1 will most likely have a wife and they live as a bonded couple. However, in this culture, it is acceptable for another warrior (Warrior 2) to place his spear outside Warrior 1's hut, indicating that the former wishes to sleep with the latter's wife, with her consent. So Warrior 2 is able to sleep with Warrior 1's wife and Warrior 1 will likely do the same with someone else's wife, as is the custom. Thus male parentage within the tribe is not clear cut because there is a possibility that one warrior's wife is carrying the offspring of another male. However, within the tribal setting, by the time children are around five or six years of age they are all communally raised.

Therefore, a warrior of this tribe may not be certain that all his wife's children are his but thinks that at least some of them will be. Furthermore, he may have a few children with other women in the tribe. Because of this, he will continue to do his best to protect the tribe and ensure that his genes and those of his close relatives will be passed on. This makes sense for the survival of his offspring. It is also interesting to note that we do not know exactly how many offspring in ancient hunter-gatherer societies were from outside the pair-bond. However, the biological complexity of adaptations for sperm competition in men and women suggests it was possibly as high as one quarter or 25 percent. It is also thought that, even in modern circumstances, up to 10 percent of children born to married couples are conceived extra-maritally.[114]

Therefore, under the hunter-gatherer tribal social structure, for which we adapted over tens of thousands of years, both male and female tribe members exercised choice with mate selection and sexuality.[115]

The Loss of Female Power and Freedom

However, with the advent of the Agricultural Revolution around 12,000 years ago, most nomadic hunter-gatherer tribes settled down in fixed locations and began growing food bearing crops. This new system of human food production spread around the world over thousands of years. This meant that now suddenly individuals owned land and property. This one major shift in human social and cultural behaviour changed the dynamic for all tribe members, especially women.[116] This is because if an individual now owned land and property, they would wish to pass this down to their offspring to ensure they had the best opportunity to survive and prosper into the future. Land represented the potential for individuals to be able to feed themselves, their children and their children's children for generations to come. Thus, receiving the land could mean the difference between life and death in these new farming communities.

On the other hand, the offspring who did not receive land, would most likely be less successful and may perish without the opportunity to farm the land and feed themselves. Therefore, under this new system it became vital for adult males to know that the children they were raising were definitely their own offspring. That is, they would not want to pass their farm to a child who was not biologically their offspring. In contrast, women knew when children were biologically theirs and were, therefore, certain that their genetics were passed on. But, males did not have this certainty if their wives had been able to mate with other male members of the community. This was considered a problem.

Now, to ensure that their genes were passed onto the next generation, the question for the land owning males became, '*How am I going to ensure that my children inherit my land?*' They concluded that the only way to be certain of their offspring's genetic line was to control female sexuality and reproduction. It was, therefore, deemed necessary to ensure that women were virgins at the time of pair-bonding and first sexual activity within this pair. In addition to implementing this new cultural code for women, men also needed to guarantee, with as much certainty as possible, that their wives did not engage in sexual relations with other males. The enforcement of these new sexual prohibitions was suddenly a survival imperative for male genes. It also resulted in the removal of rights, property ownership and many other freedoms for women, which lasted for thousands of years and in some cultures continues today. [117]

This form of suppression and control of females in human cultures was not necessary within tribal hunter-gatherer communities. However, once these cultural and social norms came into practice and were made *law*, it signalled the start of the slow road to destruction for matriarchy and feminine power. To cement the implementation of these new approaches to the feminine, many ancient religions and philosophies that honoured and respected feminine power and wisdom, had to be suppressed or destroyed. These included druidism, paganism and animism. An example of this process was evident in Christianity's mass burning of 'witches'—female midwives, nurses, herbalists, healers and other women of status and knowledge. These killings were designed to enforce the new forms of female suppression and control. [118] It has been estimated that, over the centuries, many tens of thousands of women lost their lives during this process alone. Male-driven human systems began to destroy female power and restrict female freedom to ensure that land and property were only inherited by offspring carrying the male landowner's genes. In effect, women became seen as the *property* of men. Unfortunately, this came at a great cost to us all.

However, it is important to note that, in evolutionary terms, the Agricultural Revolution is a recent event for humankind. We are still biologically, instinctively and socially adapted to our original hunter-gatherer tribal structures. Likewise, we are evolved to operate and live best within mixed power groups that respect and honour the input of both females and males, both the feminine and the masculine, in decision-making. However, this balance has been lost with the disempowerment of women at all levels of society, even though such balance is how we have naturally and, until relatively recently, successfully evolved as human beings.

This is also why we are in our current dire position as a human society, because we have removed the wise matriarchs from their roles within the collective. For example, a modern board room is typically full of young and old male 'chimpanzees' who wish to destroy the environment for short-term gain and compete against the other 'chimpanzee' males no matter the cost. Until we once again place feminine thinking in powerful decision-making positions, as we have evolved to do, we will fail to effectively address the issues we face.

The current environmental crisis is due, in large degree, to the lack of feminine power and presence in our key decision-making mechanisms. These include the arenas of political, corporate, economic, social and environmental policy and governance. Driven by an unbridled and unsustainable masculine way of thinking and acting, we are rapidly destroying the planet. To redress this situation, we must bring the masculine and the feminine back into balance as a matter of urgency by empowering women and including the feminie aspect in decision-making. The choice is a clear and achievable one. This is because, it is necessary to include the long-term thinking and nurturing care and respect for nature of the feminine to tip the scales back into humanity's favour for our future survival and that of all living beings.

Population Growth and Female Empowerment

Another key reason to re-empower and reinstate the feminine is to address the current unstainable growth in human populations around the world. As previously mentioned, our present population is over 7.7 billion people and we are predicted to reach nine billion by 2037.[119] In light of these statistics, many people say that we will never be able to deal with overpopulation and our over-breeding will doom us all. This is not true. Since peaking in the late 1960s, the percentage rate of population growth has decreased relatively consistently each year and is projected to continue decreasing.[120] Therefore, it will take us much longer to reach the nine billion mark than it did for us to achieve some of the other population milestones that have occurred in the past 100 years.

Some futurists even project that our population will likely peak at around the nine to ten billion figure. This is because it appears that improved education for women, increased choice around reproduction, contraception and family planning as well as better quality health care has had a positive effect in slowing the rate of population growth. This downward trend will continue as more girls and women on the planet gain access to universal education and greater human rights. Nonetheless, humanity as a whole has experienced staggering growth and expansion in population numbers in recent decades. In fact, there have never been more humans alive at any other point in history. This is why it is vital to rebalance the feminine to more rapidly slow our population growth now and in the future.

It seems that the reason we have a population problem to begin with is because of disempowerment of women. In every society, religion and country that chooses to empower and educate women, the reproduction rate decreases. For example, Australia, Canada, Portugal, Japan and other Western countries acknowledge that if women are empowered and educated, the population will decrease of its own accord. Women who have power and agency do not wish to be continual reproductive machines because reproduction is a biologically expensive process for women. Educated women tend to want to control their reproduction to improve life for themselves and their families. Therefore, in reality, we do not have a population problem; we have a women's empowerment problem. This and a lack of empathy and compassion for other living beings are the true sources of the problem. These core issues are, in many ways, a common theme running through our masculine-dominated humanity. This, too, will change if we can rebalance the situation.

Working with the Feminine

Within the structure of The Orangutan Project as an organisation and generally throughout my life, I work to maintain a balance between the masculine and feminine. This means that I normally don't make important decisions, travel anywhere or take major action without the influence and input of a strong woman. I do this not because I am unwilling to do so; it is more a matter of proactive choice. This is because across the masculine and feminine natures, we have evolved with two different, yet complementary types of thinking. However, as

I travel and mix within some organisational circles I observe that this balance of complementary opposites is often missing. From experience, I know that decisions made and actions taken without the valuable input of the feminine will necessarily be poorer and less effective in the long term. This is especially so because conservation and animal welfare is energetically a feminine field requiring deep understanding of sustainable, co-operative relationships and well-considered long-term planning. This is one of the core strengths and contributions of feminine thinking and something I have chosen to cultivate in many areas of my life.

For example, my wife Wendy is an exceptionally capable and strong minded woman. She brings great depth to our relationship as a counter-balance to my own strong masculine perspectives. In my working life, I have specifically sought to bring intelligent, creative and talented female co-workers onto the teams at The Orangutan Project and some of the other environmental charities we support. Furthermore, our demographic estimates reveal that around 80 to 90 percent of the loyal, generous donors and supporters of The Orangutan Project are female. We have discovered that women are more likely to understand the importance of protecting orangutans and their habitats for future generations. Indeed, they do not need convincing of the importance of this work. Additionally, when I travel to present talks and fundraising events to audiences around the world, I always look forward to an audience filled with females. If I walk into a presentation and most of the audience is male, I tend to question whether I can reach this audience. This is because, results consistently reveal that it is women who most wholeheartedly support The Orangutan Project's conservation efforts.

Additionally, in our work in the field, we have found that it is most often the local women in small communities who see the benefits of conservation for their families and the environment. This is because, according to the archetypes of Jungian psychology, nature is feminine and understanding sustainability is a feminine way of thinking. Thus, it is key to bring the women onside to ensure the longevity of our projects. As an example, if we go into an area of forest and talk to the people living there, we will engage both the men and women with an offer. We may say that we will give them some money to start a sustainable business to save the forest and that we will work with them for mutual benefit. History has shown that if we give the money to a man, he may go out the next day and buy a motorbike or a mobile phone or go out and get drunk. The next day he will wake up and say, 'Oh god, what am I going to do now?' Conversely, if we give the money to a mature woman, she will use it to start an environmentally sustainable business to support and assist the community as a whole. This type of scenario has occurred over and over again, proving that investment in women both locally and internationally benefits all concerned. The women understand the aims and values of conservation and can see long term. If we want to save an ecosystem, we need to deal with the women first and they can engage the men.

Regarding the power and ability of women in the field, I also love to share this story about one of the best performing Wildlife Protection Teams. Most in the West assume that Indonesia is a male-dominated culture and that women are not accorded power in the working arena. We have supported many wildlife protection units that are largely composed of young macho men who go out into the forest to defend the wildlife and protect the best interests of the habitat and environment. This may mean that they come up against illegal hunters, poachers and loggers; it is difficult and challenging work. However, the best group we have ever had was led by a five-foot-tall young woman. Interestingly, the men, who would usually compete with male leaders, would simply listen and accept the feminine power she used in her role. She was not a threat to these young men's masculinity and they respected her authority in the role. Thus she was both a highly effective and valued leader.

I have also come to understand that a well-adjusted man is not threatened by a strong woman or her feminine power. Quite the reverse is true, as it is much easier for a man who is comfortable within his masculinity to work alongside the feminine. In my experience, it is generally dysfunctional women who dislike men or dysfunctional men who are insecure around women, because each have problems balancing the masculine and feminine power bases. Conversely, well-adjusted people do not struggle with this as it is natural and beneficial for all concerned. Perhaps those who are unable or unwilling to work together in this way are facing an attitudinal issue? It seems counter-productive to allow those with poor attitudes, who feel threatened and who wish to reduce another's power, to retain control and make important decisions that affect us all. In fact, it is detrimental and dangerous, and therefore must change.

Rebalancing the Feminine

'It is not the strongest of the species that survive, nor the most intelligent, but those most responsive to change.'
Charles Darwin

It is time for us to redress the balance and bring back into equilibrium both masculine and feminine input. This translates at all levels of our societies, organisations, governments, communities and homes. We can do this by respecting and valuing the contribution of the feminine, not as better than or superior to the masculine, but of as equal merit and complementary strength. Most importantly, because we will all do better as a whole when we do so.

Natural Balance

Balance is a natural state. By disempowering the feminine and removing it from its intrinsic place within our cultures, we have put ourselves out of balance with disastrous consequences. We have all suffered—the masculine, the feminine, the environment and all other living beings. This began when the imbalanced masculine force of production, competition, expansion, reward and short-term thinking was no longer tempered by the more nurturing, distribution focused, conservative, sustainable, long-term approach of the feminine. This is evidenced by the following sobering statistics within human societies in which we are told that hunger and poverty are humanitarian crises. However, these could just as well be considered as a lack of the feminine aspect, where distribution and ensuring everyone has enough are prime imperatives, instead of the masculine drive to produce and compete at all costs.

1. Currently across the globe we are now producing more calories per person than at any other time in history. Yet people are still starving and suffering from mal-nutrition right at this moment. The truth is that we have the capacity to feed the entire world today if we chose to do so. [121]

2. Researchers estimate that approximately 11.3 percent of the world's population are termed as 'hungry.' This means that roughly 805 million people are undernourished on a daily basis and consume less than the recommended 2,100 calories per day. [122]

3. At the same time, it is estimated that approximately 45 million people in the USA go on a diet each year, spending around $33 billion USD on diets and diet products. [123] Based upon these statistics, it is considered that these funds could easily contribute towards putting an end to world hunger.

Decision Making

By suppressing the feminine, we have destroyed our ability to make good decisions and create long-term strategies to serve all parts of our societies. We have been operating with a lopsided perspective, leading to perverse outcomes that have potentially taken us to the brink of our own survival. This is because when either the masculine or the feminine is excluded from the decision-making process, we lose our ability to reach a balance between competition and survival of the fittest, and the long-term health and wellbeing of the community. Much like two houses of parliament, the masculine and feminine represent two different ways of seeing and experiencing the world. It is only through the use of both of these separate power bases that we achieve the best decisions. Therefore, we need to go through both 'houses' to attain a more informed, balanced and holistic way of understanding the world. One is not better than the other nor should one rule and one serve. It is not a case of them against us; instead, we need each other to create the best way forwards as a species.

Sustainable Long Term Future

Ultimately we need the balance of the masculine and the feminine for our own long-term survival. With the aggressive, progress based, win-at-all-costs approach of the masculine, we have been waging a war that nature has been losing as we have wielded our technological advancements to tame and control it. Without the feminine, we have lacked the cooperative, cohesive and sustainable perspective required to protect and revere Mother Nature as the ancient philosophical traditions of the animists, once did. It is now time for the feminine aspects of nature conservation, environmental care and animal welfare to be brought back into balance to the benefit of all living beings. To solve the problems of the world, this must be done sooner rather than later—we have nothing to lose and everything to gain.

Beware of Becoming the Monster You Fight

As part of a leadership team at one stage in my career, I had the experience of working with what I can only describe as a female leader who was operating from a masculine perspective. She was a strong, outspoken feminist who saw herself as something of a suffragette who in her own way was facing down the tyranny of the patriarchy. As a committed campaigner for women's rights, she was also firmly anti-sexist and made a point of confronting any sexist behaviour in the workplace, which made perfect sense to me and I supported this initiative. However, this leader was unable to successfully interact with or relate to equally strong, self-respecting men. As a result, she eliminated almost all the male executives and replaced them with like-minded women, leaving one relatively weak and compliant male remaining on the executive board.

As I observed the shifts that were occurring within the company, it was not lost on me, nor perhaps on the others who worked with this organisation, that our female leader was behaving in a markedly sexist manner. Moreover, she was doing so in the name of an egalitarian feminist philosophy whereby we were all to be treated as equal. For me, her behaviour demonstrated the danger of becoming the monster we fight—in her crusade to fight against sexism, injustice and patriarchy, she began to display these traits herself. It is always the way that we become the monster that we fight when we view ourselves as victims, cultivating a mentality of justifiable rage and indignant opposition towards the forces that we perceive are victimising us. In this dynamic, there is always a sense of them against us, victim against persecutor and, in this case, men against women.

However our actions and results will always lead us down the path to becoming a monster if we view ourselves and others from these polarising perspectives. This is because, by doing so we place ourselves firmly in the realm of opposing pairs and are therefore unable to see past our own prejudices and judgements. Importantly, when we see ourselves as either a victim or a righteous crusader against the perceived oppressor, we often give ourselves an excuse for very bad behaviour. In fact, we begin to put back out into the world the very thing we fight against. Thus, the victim becomes the monster and the vigilante falls into the same trap. We will always create a lop-sided result if we come from a lop-sided perspective. This is because we are unable to see beyond our inner imbalance and, as such, are unable to transcend our own story.

This is a simple cautionary tale, but one which is always timely, especially within the arenas of conservation and animal welfare: remember to beware the monsters you fight as you may end up becoming one.

The Parable of the Snake and the Sage

In contrast to the previous story, in which we can become the monster we fight, it is also vital that we do not treat ourselves as less than others. As the parable below encourages us to not only maintain love and compassion for all, but for ourselves as well. This is because extending compassion towards others, does not mean that we lose our strength of will nor sense of our own worth. However, if we can balance the striving nature of the masculine with the nurturing care of the feminine we can maintain informed and active compassion.

One day a wise old sage was travelling through a village. Along his way he was informed by the children of the village that there was a wily snake living in the nearby field which liked to terrorise and bite the youngsters. As the sage knew the snake well, he sought him out to scold his serpent friend for his behaviour. He instructed the snake to stop biting the children and do no harm to others, telling the snake, "You should love your fellow beings." The snake agreed to abide by the sage's advice and the sage bid his friend farewell and continued on his journey.

Over time the local children noticed that the snake was no longer aggressive and threatening towards them, however they were still afraid of him. Taking advantage of the situation the children began to treat the peaceful snake badly. They threw stones at him from afar and, when close, picked him up by the tail and mercilessly beat his body against the ground. Yet the snake did not bite them nor fight back against this behaviour.

Sometime later the sage returned to the village and enquired about his old friend, the snake. However no one had seen or heard from him for a time. The sage walked to the field to look for the snake and finally found his friend cowering under a bush. Weak, bruised, battered and close to death the snake was a shadow of his previous self.

Feeling pity for the snake the sage asked, "What happened?" The snake replied, "Teacher, I did as you told me and did no harm to others." "You fool!" The sage replied, "I told you not to bite, but I never told you not to hiss!"124 "You should love your fellow beings, however you should be careful how you express that love."

The parable of the snake and the sage illustrates that being truly loving is not the same as being weak and down trodden, as the snake chose to be when he failed to scare away his attackers with a hiss. Neither is being loving found in the need for pleasing others or having others to like and approve of you. As such, an unintelligent approach to love will always fall short of our expectations especially if we give love as a way of receiving something back in return.

In this story, the snake became weak and un-snake like by thinking he was doing the good thing to allow his mistreatment. In his weakness, he enabled the children to behave cruelly without bringing this to their attention. Therefore the key lies in intelligently expressing our love and compassion for others and maintaining a balance between the head and the heart and masculine and feminine aspects. In fact, being proactively good and standing firm in the middle-path may not make everyone happy, however it will always result in the greatest outcome for all involved.

Chapter Nine
Transcendence

'We know what we are, but know not what we may be.'
William Shakespeare

Ultimately the journey to find our humanity is one of transcendence. Whilst the concept has been contemplated by philosophers, scholars and spiritual seekers across the millennia, transcendence is often approached in terms of other-worldliness and divinity. However, when I use the term I refer to it as a state of going beyond. In fact, the etymology of transcendence is composed of the following: *"The Latin prefix "trans" meaning "beyond," and the word "scandare" meaning "to climb." When you achieve transcendence, you have gone beyond ordinary limitations."* [125] Therefore, instead of it being an intangible idea outside the reach of comprehension, it is something that we can each understand and apply. Importantly, the benefits of this state are practical and available for us all. Firstly, as individuals, we can transcend our biological, instinctive and cultural drives. Secondly, on the collective level, we can go beyond the arbitrary ways we separate ourselves from each other by ethnicity, nationality, belief, gender, status, age, creed or preference, and where we perceive ourselves as separate from other living beings. This is where true humanity lies.

For me, this is best explained in two parts.

The Transcendent Path

1. As part of our material existence, we live in a world where we encounter pairs of polar opposites, such as up/down, in/out, east/west, day/night, masculine/feminine, happy/sad, good/evil, love/hate, birth/death, the list is endless. When we encounter these opposites, we experience a state known as dualism. The presence of one aspect defines the absence of the other and we do not experience both at the same time. We can oscillate between these two opposing states in a constant dance of lopsidedness: one or the other, never both. In this dualistic existence there is also necessarily a sense of separation because each opposite is distinct from the other. For example, when we look out our window there will always be north or south, east or west, light or dark, day time or night time; we will encounter one of these at a time. However, when we reach beyond the dualistic nature of everyday life we can see past or transcend these opposites.

2. At this point, we experience the transcendence or shift in perspective to wholeness and a view beyond dualism. For example, what if we could leave the planet and view the Earth from outer space? All we could see would be the blue-green planet we call home spinning through space. Suddenly, we could grasp the bigger picture of life on Earth and experience the concept of wholeness all at once. Instead of the opposites of east and west, north and south, we could see all at the same time. From this perspective, there would be no opposite, only a reconciliation and unity of the planet as one.

At the same time, we understand that back on Earth these opposites still exist, however we would see beyond them as we take in the full picture. In this way, we transcend the bounds of Earth to see the totality of the oneness to which we are blind in our everyday lives. However, would anything have changed back on planet Earth? No, we have simply been able to see beyond our human limitations to a greater truth. This is a transcendent way of seeing and the good news is that it can be applied to all areas of understanding.

Astronauts and those who have had the opportunity to travel out of Earth's biosphere into space often recount the experience of seeing their home planet from this vantage point as a life-changing, transcendent moment. They have seen beyond the arbitrary segregations that we impose upon ourselves and these divisions lose their meaning once viewed from this perspective. Instead of seeing separate countries and independent states, these space travellers have observed the truth of the unity and wholeness in front of them. Land and oceans extending around the planet, meeting without border or separation as part of the globe we call home. Seeing the world in this way is like switching an internal camera lens from close-up to extreme wide angle. This transcendent perspective reveals a beauty and oneness and it changes everything. Some refer to this change as the '*overview effect*', a term coined in 1987 by space philosopher Frank White to describe the mental shift of astronauts when they experience the Earth as part of a larger whole.[126]

> "*There are no borders or boundaries on our planet, except those that we create with our minds and human behaviours.*"
> Frank White

Likewise within the rainforests of Borneo and Sumatra where we conduct eco tours to orangutan habitats, we can see the duality of life all around us. There is birth and death, abundance and scarcity, the wet season and the dry, predator and the prey, growth and decay and the beauty of life and the struggle for survival. Within the depths of the forest it is a hot, humid and challenging environment, however when we step back and see it in its entirety, it is a radiantly beautiful place. It is from this transcendent view of the rainforest that the gift of nature's sacredness is available to experience and is something which cannot be taught, but only felt in the moment. Again, this is why many of our eco tour participants say they are life- changing experiences, as they get to see beyond their everyday lives into a more holistic version of life.

At the level of our inner selves, transcendence can be experienced when we go beyond our dualistic state of being to appreciate the greater truth awaiting us. For example, we can oscillate between feelings of love or hate. However, when we transcend these opposing, transient emotions, we can appreciate both simultaneously, going beyond these to 'become love.' This experience of love means that we don't 'feel love' or 'give love' in the usual conditional way, instead we are love. In turn, love flows unconditionally from us and this is what others experience in our presence. Likewise, with the dualistic opposites of good and bad, to transcend these we perceive both aspects at the same time to become good. In this way, 'goodness' is our way of being in the world and from this state, goodness flows. The same approach can be applied the opposites of happy and sad, where we integrate both and become *happiness*. This means that we no longer seek happiness outside ourselves as we understand that it resides with us, in the transcendent state. Correspondingly, happiness flows from us as we wish others to be happy also. Therefore, transcendence is both a practical and powerful way of perceiving and experiencing life.

A close shave with my own mortality helped me to experience the possibility of transcending the fear of death.

Leptospirosis

After a site visit to BTP, Sumatra in 2017, I arrived back home to Perth with what I assumed was a case of the flu. I let my wife, Wendy, know that I wasn't feeling 100 percent at the time and we both put my ill health down to simple 'man flu.' Not giving it much further thought, I continued to focus on my responsibilities with The Orangutan Project during the following days. However, instead of easing, my symptoms became steadily worse, progressing from muscle aches and chills to the point that one morning I could not get out of bed. I felt exhausted and extremely unwell.

At the same time, Wendy was getting ready for work. Before leaving for the day she came in to say goodbye. I remember realising in that moment that perhaps this wasn't a simple case of the flu and there was something more serious going on with my health. I relayed this information to Wendy and suggested that she take me to the local doctor straight away. However, in her rush to ensure she would not be late for work, she quickly assessed the situation and concluded that I was exaggerating my condition, as men tend to do when they have man flu. She told me, like a true Australian country girl, to "Toughen up princess;" she would see me when she returned home in the afternoon.

I stayed in bed in the hope that I would feel better as the morning went on, but I did not. As I lay there, I experienced the sensations of what I would later learn were my kidneys slowly shutting down and my heart beating irregularly, sending waves of dizziness surging through my brain. Even as I felt these bodily sensations, my thoughts were strangely peaceful. This sense of peace increased as time passed. I had the dual experience of the approach of death and a detached inner calm. The one thought that arose within me was incomprehension at why humans continued to destroy the pure beauty of nature and the lives of other living beings. This was combined with an unreconciled desire to help change the situation in humanity and for nature. With this thought *came a deep sense of sadness yet I wasn't afraid of death. I was more disappointed that I hadn't completed the work I set out to do.*

At this point something roused me from my delirious state and back to consciousness. I knew I had to get myself to the doctor, and fast. Crawling out of bed, I made way to the garage, into our car and managed to drive myself to the local doctor. When I staggered into the reception area, the nurse on duty took one look at me and hurried me into the doctor's treatment room. After a few questions and a brief assessment, the doctor said, "I am not even going to try and treat you. You need to go straight to hospital." I contacted my father, who was available to pick me up and take me to the nearest emergency department, where they confirmed that I was close to death and required urgent treatment.

The hospital staff also insisted that I be kept under strict quarantine as they did not know if what I had contracted was contagious at this stage. Once my medical tests were returned, it was determined that I had an advanced case of leptospirosis. This is a sometimes fatal bacterial infection that can be contracted from contact with infected food, water or animals. It causes kidney failure, breathing difficulties, irregular heart rates and meningitis (inflammation of the lining of the brain.) My case was so severe that had I gone untreated for a few more hours, I would likely have died at home alone in bed.

When reflecting upon the experience and the realisation that I was brought close to death by this disease, it struck me that the dying process was not so bad after all. Plus, I had faced a similar experience once before, in a rainforest in Borneo. I had no fear of dying per se- I had perhaps transcended my emotional reactions to the physical 'death stupor' experience. However, what most stood out in my mind was the idea that humans still had a way to go before we understood that our destruction of nature and living beings was so harmful, not just to other life forms, but to us as well. From the perspective of a near death experience, it seemed so pointless and so equally avoidable. What I felt in those moments in which I considered my own mortality was not fear, anger or hate, but an overriding love and compassion for those I would leave behind and those I was yet to help. For it is always love that is the key principle behind the work we do. Love always is and always will be at the heart of everything; this is the truth of what connects us all.

As you may imagine, Wendy was horrified to receive the call at work to inform her of my admission to hospital and serious medical condition. She rushed to be by my side in hospital and nursed me through the following weeks as I regained my health and strength. I think that will be the last time either of us underestimates a deceptively harmless case of man flu.

Intriguingly, I also believe that this event revealed to me the manner in which perhaps almost every orangutan which has ever lived, prior to the arrival of humans into their territories, would have died. As everything that lives ultimately dies and the rainforest teaches us this so eloquently with its natural cycle of birth and death. Therefore, I can only imagine how it may be for an orangutan who is old, injured or sick as it senses the approach of death. However, I would suggest the orangutan would make its final night nest in their tree top home, resting there as the life-force wanes. Its senses would begin to shut down and the activity of life replaced by an inner peace. A peace in which they are somehow still present whilst consciousness disappears and the life force leaves the body. For me, the physical sensations of the death stupor were like falling peacefully into conscious presence beyond personality, a calm place of rest, a state which awaits us all.

'I saw in this reaper a vision of death, but in this death nothing is sad, it takes place in broad daylight with a sun that floods everything with the light of fine gold.'
Vincent Van Gogh

The Transcendence Paradox

In addition to helping us to move beyond the dualistic perspective, transcendence can allow us to begin to see the paradox of wholeness within the opposite parts. We are then able to simultaneously *appreciate the good within the bad and the bad within the good* yet see each as one. The perfect example of this is demonstrated in the classic Taoist symbol of the yin and yang, mentioned earlier in the chapter on the masculine and the feminine. It is traditionally drawn as a circle containing two complementary black and white teardrop shapes, with the head of one teardrop facing up and the other facing downwards. They completely fill the circle with their complementary shapes. However, within the white teardrop, is a black spot and within the black teardrop is a white spot. These symbolise the opposite existing within its complement. That is, within each good action there is a seed of bad and within each bad action there is a seed of good, yet oneness is present at the same time.

For example, amidst the horror and destruction of World War II there also great feats of heroism, compassion and perseverance. Furthermore from the hindsight of today, we know that once World War II was over, it became the catalyst for the relative peace humans now experience worldwide. In fact, the historical period from the end of World War II in 1945 to the present day has been coined the "*long peace*", and is unprecedented.[127] This is discussed in Steve Pinker's book, "*The Better Angels of Our Nature*," in which he examines evidence demonstrating that across the globe, crime, violence and war have decreased and are continuing to do so. [128] Although, for many of us, this may not be our subjective experience, because with increased global communication, violence and conflict of the world is projected into our living rooms each day. Nevertheless, the statistics from the global perspective, show less crime, violence and a reduction in war across our growing population. It appears that the pain and suffering of the past has resulted in greater peace and stability in the present.[129] However, I will add that this is in no way to disregard the pain and hardship endured by those individuals and nations which have experienced the ravages of war during this period.

On the other hand, within great happiness can also exist the seed of sadness. For example, the arrival of a new puppy into the home first it brings the joy of love and companionship as the pet becomes a much-loved member of the family. However, this puppy will also one day grow old and die. At this point there will be the grief of loss and the sadness of missing this beloved pet. With transcendence, however, we can go beyond this duality to see the pairs of opposites making up the whole, to appreciate the good within the bad and the bad within the good. This takes us beyond the realm of duality on Earth as there is ultimately goodness, joy and love in perceiving the whole.

How can we apply transcendence to go beyond our current ways of being?

Applying Transcendence

Biology and Culture

As a species, humans evolved within an environment where we were competing against nature to survive and succeed. We required food, water, shelter, warmth and an environment which could provide us with these basic elements. As tribal hunter-gatherers, we considered nature as endlessly vast, unpredictable and powerful in comparison with ourselves as biological organisms. Due to this, our biology has been combative and competitive, always struggling to survive life as a small part of the enormity of nature. This approach to nature was appropriate-necessary, even- whilst we were living in small populations without the benefits of technology, mechanisation and massive industrial growth. However, as we gained power over our food supply with the Agricultural Revolution and then over much of nature itself with the Industrial Revolution, a seismic power shift occurred. This power fell into our inexperienced hands, exacerbated by the disempowerment of feminine wisdom which connected us to nature and sustainability. We have not yet evolved the wisdom to handle the great power that we now wield over the planet and all living beings. In fact, we are still operating from our originally successful evolutionary adaptations which were viable when we were simply hunter-gatherers. Therein lies the problem.

We now have the capability and the drive to control nature on a planetary scale, yet our biological operating systems were designed before we could imagine such power. In this way, humanity is like a child playing with multiple nuclear bombs. We could end our existence in a moment, but in many ways we are still not cognisant that we hold this power. Therefore, our task must be to transcend our biology and our cultural behaviours for our own survival and that of other living beings. Currently, our biological and cultural drives are both interactive and intertwined and are still set to hunter-gatherer mode, rather than to that of good planetary stewardship. The key for us lies in our ability to appreciate the dualistic opposites of nature or progress, environment or survival, humans or other living beings, and go beyond these to embrace the oneness of all life. In order for us to understand that our survival is linked to the survival of the whole, we must transcend our biological and cultural programming.

'The more one forgets oneself—by giving oneself to a cause to serve or another person to love—the more human they are and the more they actualizes themselves. Self-actualization is possible only as a side-effect of self-transcendence.'
Victor Frankl

Ego-Self

On the individual level, our ability to transcend relies on our willingness to go beyond our attachment to the conscious ego-self and our sub conscious drives. As discussed in an earlier chapter, these aspects of our psyches govern much of our instinctive and reactive ways of thinking and acting. Additionally, these aspects are generally what we identify with as our personality selves or who we are. Therefore, to free ourselves from reactive emotion, childhood memories and habitual thought patterns, we need to go beyond these inner drivers. We can do this by transcending our conscious ego-self and sub conscious self to embrace our greater non-personal *Self* of the spirit. This is where expanded consciousness, resides, combined with the awareness that we are all connected. This, in turn, opens us to the experience of oneness, love, compassion, joy and happiness. In many philosophical and spiritual traditions this is called the path of the middle way and self-realisation in which we are able to simultaneously see the opposing parts of ourselves as well as the larger whole. This is a state where the head and heart merge in a wisdom beyond the limitations of the human intellect. Then we can transcend our ego and sub conscious selves to experience our true Self.

How can we go beyond our smaller, separate aspects of self to experience our true Self?

Drowning in a Sea of Love

My initial encounter with my *true Self* began with an event, which if it hadn't happened to me, I would perhaps have not believed it myself. It both surprised and amazed me with its simple beauty. But at the time, I had no idea that an encounter such as this could exist. As I reflect upon that time all those years ago, I can appreciate that this experience changed me in a subtle way and set in place a chain of circumstances that altered the course my life would take. This was because it opened my heart and mind to a different reality, one which gave me a tantalising glimpse beyond everyday existence. Once it was over I continued on for many years in almost in the same way as I had prior to it happening. However I realise this event planted a seed within me. As we know, when suitably nurtured, seeds germinate and grow as nature intends. Therefore, it was only a matter of time until this seed would grow, blossom and bear fruit in my life.

The beginning of my journey to, what some call, the opening of the heart or experience of the true Self, happened when I was around 12 years old. At the time, my family was living in the bustling cosmopolitan city of Hong Kong. We had left Australia and settled there when I was just 18 months old because Dad had been offered an overseas position with the company for which he worked at the time. As such, I had basically grown up in this unique East Asian environment.

During my childhood, I remember that for some reason alongside my regular activities of attending school, hanging out with friends, playing sport and spending time with my numerous pets, I would often meditate alone in my room. My parents were what I can best describe as agnostic. This meant that although they probably believed in some form of higher power or creative organising energy in the universe, they had no particular religious affiliations, practices or beliefs- neither did they meditate. However, for me, meditating was something that felt natural, normal and innately attractive. Upon reflection, perhaps this was because I grew up in a culture in which the major spiritual and philosophical traditions included Shenism (Chinese Folk Religion) Buddhism, Confucianism and Taoism. In these religions, some forms of mediation were often practiced by followers. Therefore, I can't say whether I chose to meditate of my own volition or learned to mediate by absorbing this practice from my cultural background, but it was a part of my life from an early age.

My meditation practice consisted of ensuring that I had un-interrupted time during which I would sit comfortably, close my eyes, calm my breath and bring my attention within. From this point I would explore consciousness, letting myself go into the void of my inner landscape where I found deep peace and tranquility. On one such occasion, seemingly no different from any other, I began to ponder on the concept of God. I had heard of God as an idea yet had no practical understanding of who or what God was. I allowed this question to sit within my consciousness and from within me arose a clear desire to meet God. At this point, I recall posing a request to the void within, asking to see and know God. I was not specifically expecting a response but was open to receiving one. I suddenly became overwhelmed because in what seemed like an instant, everything shifted.

What happened next is difficult to put into words because the experience was beyond any form of human perception that I had ever encountered. What I can say, in the somewhat ungainly and inadequate form of my English vocabulary, is that it was like dying in a sea of love. The part of me that was 'me' disappeared into this sea; 'I' as a form or concept no longer existed nor held meaning. The experience was of boundless expansiveness. There were no barriers nor end to this ocean of love of which I was now a part. To say it was like drowning would come close, yet I was drowning in true beauty, true love. There was no sadness and no feeling of regret at losing myself. In fact, the reverse was true and a love and peace and bliss beyond all understanding engulfed me.

It was as if I had melted into 'presence,' so the experience, for want of a more accurate word, was all there was. I felt no time, no space, no separation- nothing, except love. Even when I recall this event I am brought to tears and rendered speechless. Yet, these are not tears of sadness but of recognition and joy at the memory. Much like when a person finds themselves in the presence of unconditional love or comprehends a deep universal truth for the first time, involuntary tears of recognition well up from within. Speech fails and words are but poor substitutes to use to describe the all-encompassing nature of the experience.

I don't know how long I was in this state. However, as I became aware that I was beginning to leave it, I felt the weight of body consciousness returning. At the same moment, my mind started to try to turn this perception into a logical experience. Essentially, it is beyond the concept of the mind so it was impossible to categorise and classify an event of this nature. Instead I struggled to hold on and tried to return to the indescribable lightness of being that I had experienced. But, this grasping to hold on only pulled me further from the boundless state. I felt caught in this strange midway point of coming out of the experience yet struggling to return. The weird part about it was (and I know this is going to sound crazy) I had the thought that I didn't want to go back to body consciousness and material life. I wanted to always remain in this state, immersed in the sea of love. Immediately as this thought surfaced these words came straight to me in response; "It's not your time yet." It was a strangely purposeful reply.

That is all I remember. I opened my eyes to find myself sitting in my bedroom with those words reverberating through my being. Everything in the external world of my room looked the same yet also appeared strangely enlivened. But something within me had changed. I had been given a glimpse into life's underlying reality, into another way of being and I yearned to return to this place once more. At the same time, I also felt an overwhelming sense of gratitude that I had been gifted this state of expanded awareness and had felt the essence of complete oneness. I knew this experience was extraordinary, but had few words to describe it. The truth was, at the tender age of 12, I could never un-know this state nor forget this experience.

My unexpected encounter had given me a taste of something far beyond ordinary existence. However, much like the dual aspect of the double-edged sword, whilst I treasured this experience as a gift I also felt a sense of loss. From then onwards, I became strangely aware I was missing something. It would be some time before I found this presence again. Yet in the meantime my life progressed much as before. Initially, I continued with my own form of quiet contemplation practice when and where I could. During this time, I was never able to regain the same level of deep connection with oneness I had encountered earlier. This did not deter me from my inner journey, as to my young mind I had stumbled upon something that was achingly intangible, but also, somehow more real to me than my material everyday life.

I did not share my experience with family or friends and kept my inner explorations to myself. They were indescribably precious and any attempt to put them into words could only fall short of their beauty and truth. Thus, it remained as part of my own private universe and I travelled there when I could. Interestingly, it would be another inner experience that would bring a halt to my practice and cause me to cease my journeying for many years. That experience was my biological coming of age, the process of adolescence.

Puberty arrived as I hit my teenage years, marking the start of a dramatic physical and mental shift in both my inner and outer worlds. With its rapid onset, I experienced the effects of surges of testosterone and a range of other hormonal changes. My young boyish brain was rewired for the path to adulthood and new desires, urges and preoccupations took over my life, as happens with any adolescent. Correspondingly my body grew and developed at a staggering rate. This new hormonally driven aspect of myself increased the strength of my personality and I became aware of a strong sense of individuality evolving inside my psyche. When my family and I returned to Australia from Hong Kong, I was already 15 years of age and right in the middle of this pivotal transformation.

We settled into a home in the quiet suburban area of Bull Creek, approximately 20 minutes outside Western Australia's capital city, Perth. One day whilst quietly contemplating in my room, I suddenly felt my personality fall into what I could only term as a void. In this seemingly vast, deep nothingness I felt that 'I' was being stripped away, that an important part of me was dying. Unfortunately, at this time in my life, my adolescent personality was too strong to allow what was happening to occur. Instead of recognizing the void, as my own Self -as pure love and joy- a great fear beyond anything I had ever experienced came over me. Gripped by this intense fear and terrified at the loss of my personality I pulled my consciousness out of the void as quickly as I could. Dazed and startled by what I had experienced, I was shaken to the core of my being by this encounter and it was some time until the fear of the void would die down within me. I had no understanding of what had just occurred and did not wish to experience this sensation again any time soon.

From this point, it would be a long time before I would return to the inner journey and my path. However, once the turmoil of growing up had passed, life offered me another pathway when my teacher (Guru) arrived. Through his teachings he blessed me with the knowledge which has allowed the inherent love and joy that exists in all of us to be brought into consciousness and integrated into my life's work. I hope that in a small way this book holds for you the 'ring of truth' – that is, knowledge that you have somehow always known has now been brought into your consciousness with love and joy.

Epilogue
A Way Forward

'A good life is one inspired by love and guided by knowledge.'
Bertrand Russell

As I write this, I am on my way to East Kalimantan, Indonesia to host an eco-tour for supporters and donors of The Orangutan Project. These are compassionate and concerned people just like you. We will be visiting rainforests, a national park and rehabilitation and reintroduction centres to see orangutans in the wild as well as those who are on their way to being released to freedom. We will also be fortunate enough to experience the beauty and magnificence of the natural jungle environments of the area. Each of these aspects affirm that we are effectively working towards some positive solutions for our orangutan cousins. However, the situation is still urgent for all species of orangutan, especially the Tapanuli orangutan that I mentioned in the Introduction. We still have a way to go in our work to save our orange friends. There is a way forward in which we can each make a difference and help to change the situation for the orangutans and all living beings, however, our actions cannot remain as they have been before.

Our way into the future must be led by the light of our greater humanity, a humanity that is informed by the understanding that we are each part of the web of life, the oneness of existence. In finding our own humanity we are now capable of recognising it within other living beings, our great ape cousins included, and in life itself. Our species is intelligent, aware, adaptive and innovative. Due to this, we are capable of both staggering destruction and acts of deep wisdom and immense compassion. The journey forward must begin now, as we proactively choose to follow the latter path. Humans are not our biology. We are not our culture or our hunter-gatherer tribal past. We are each much more than these limited definitions and can transcend them so that we can make the necessary changes.

To do this we need to be part of the process as individuals and work together with others to offer our support and a more balanced way of seeing, thinking and acting within the world. Instead of focusing upon the false dichotomy of *people versus wildlife, conservation versus progress, the environment versus profit, them versus us* and being paralysed by these seeming conflicts of interest. We need to see that there is an alternative way forward. One which transcends current thinking and which engages the wisdom of a balanced heart and head, creative and logical ways of solving problems and embraces a more compassionate and humane approach to all life on Earth. As a pure heart is transcendental and sees beyond our conditioning. Additionally, with this new way of balanced thinking we can become more effective and our actions more lasting to help our fellow living beings.

We also know that by looking after others and doing good we are helping ourselves as well as others at the same time. In this way, everyone wins and there is a greater result across all fronts. The way of compassionate, right action is a natural expression of love that is no burden for us. In this transcendent way of being there is also no sacrifice and nothing lost for the individual. Our new definition of humanity is not just about what you do in the world which makes a difference, but who you are being whilst you do it. May we each move forward with the compassion, empathy, kindness and generosity of spirit of which we are all capable and open our hearts and minds to experience the possibilities that our humanity offers us all.

> 'What humans do over the next 50 years will determine
> the fate of all life on the planet.'
> Sir David Attenborough

Lighting the Way

I have been visiting the scenic, biodiverse wetland areas along the Sekonyer River in Borneo for over 25years now. This riverine region meanders through some of the last remaining sections of lush, green, pristine rainforest in the area. It is home to an amazing array of wildlife, including orangutans, proboscis monkeys, macaques, crocodiles, a myriad of bird and insect life and rare pink river dolphins living wild and free. It is a place of overwhelming beauty and grace, teaming with life in its many unique forms. This makes it a popular destination for eco tours into orangutan habitat.

However, one of the region's most popular experiences is an evening river cruise through the nipa palm areas, where the river becomes brackish from the salt of the sea. These are home to the native firefly species known locally as 'kunang kunang.' Each night along the river, the rainforest vegetation is lit up by these tiny bioluminescent beings, which are not flies at all, but soft-bodied beetles related to the glow-worm, scattered throughout the trees and bushes fringing the river. [130] These insects use their light to lure prey or attract mates, and are a true wonder of nature. They are indescribably beautiful and almost magical in their incandescence. The experience of seeing the fireflies shining their soft light into the evening darkness is literally breathtaking.

When I was first fortunate enough to experience this phenomenon all those years ago, the vegetation along the river banks was lit up like hundreds of highly decorated Christmas trees. The numbers and concentration of these remarkable fireflies were so large that their mass clusters of glowing bodies filled the trees for long stretches on either side *of the river. It was a sight to behold. However, as I returned over the years, I noticed a decline - gradual at first, but soon more rapid - of these luminous insects. Now instead of the massed clusters of lights which used to grace the riverbanks, there are more thinly scattered groups and sometimes even dark gaps amongst the trees. With such a visibly obvious being as the firefly, it has been relatively easy to note the loss of their once large populations as well as their diminishing presence.*

Local conservation and tourist organisations have observed the decline of the fireflies. Factors such as destruction of their habitat for palm oil (a form of unsustainable monoculture), pollution, pesticides and human activity have all been blamed for the situation. In some ways, it appears that the fireflies are reflecting an environmental litmus test for the health of the surrounding ecosystems. Such areas are also home to wild orangutans, who are similarly suffering due to these impacts. In this way, the fireflies play a role in clearly showing us that our actions are not without effects on other living beings. Living beings which share nature's beauty with us and have a right to be here on planet Earth, just as we do. We are each connected as part of life itself.

However, there is another way of viewing the gift that the fireflies bring and perhaps they can act as a pointer for our way forward? Whenever I witness the spectacle of these luminous beings against the darkness of the Bornean rainforest, I am reminded of the spark of humanity that resides within each one of us. The fireflies shine their inner light for all to see and they do this each night as an intrinsic part of who and what they are as living beings. In fact, the fireflies cannot help but share their inner light, as this naturally shines out from within them. In doing so, they create such visual beauty and wonder in the world as a by-product of their existence. They are light.

Correspondingly, my hope for the future is that we could each choose to extend our humanity outwards to all living beings, understanding their value and worth and respecting their right to live safe, wild and free. I hope that we can shine our individual lights, add our support to conservation organisations that do good work and join together to make the changes and take the steps that we all know are necessary. It is not too late to create these shifts and together, we can make a difference if we act with intelligence and compassion. Now is the time to find our humanity, to transcend our biology, culture and tribal past, and spread the light of true humanity into the world. There is no time to waste.

The choice is yours, what will you decide?

Leif Cocks
2019

Notes

Introduction

1   Stokstad, Eric. *New Great Ape Species Found Sparking Fears for its Survival.* Science Magazine. 2017

2   Davis, Nicola. *New Species of Orangutan Discovered in Sumatra.* The Guardian, Australian Ed. 2017

3   Batang Toru. *Introducing Sumatra's New Great Ape Species.* www.batangtoru.org/orangutan/

4   Davis, Nicola. *New Species of Orangutan Discovered in Sumatra.* The Guardian, Australian Ed. 2017

5   Davis, Nicola. *New Species of Orangutan Discovered in Sumatra.* The Guardian, Australian Ed. 2017

6   Batang Toru. *Introducing Sumatra's New Great Ape Species.* www.batangtoru.org/orangutan/

7   Batang Toru. *Introducing Sumatra's New Great Ape Species.* www.batangtoru.org/orangutan/

8   Stokstad, Eric. *New Great Ape Species Found Sparking Fears for its Survival.* Science Magazine. 2017

9   Batang Toru. *Introducing Sumatra's New Great Ape Species.* www.batangtoru.org/orangutan/

10   International Union for the Conservation of Nature. *Red List 2018* www.iucnredlist.org

11   International Union for the Conservation of Nature. *Red List 2018.* www.iucnredlist.org/

12   International Union for the Conservation of Nature. *Red List 2018.* www.iucnredlist.org/

13   Dell' Amore, Christine. *Species Extinction Happening 100 Times Faster Because of Humans?* National Geographic. 2014

14   Dell' Amore, Christine. *Species Extinction Happening 100 Times Faster Because of Humans?* National Geographic. 2014

15   Bar-On, Yinon, Rob Phillips, and Ron Milo. *The Bio Mass Distribution on Earth.* PNAS. 2018 www.pnas.org/content/115/25/6506

16   Bar-On, Yinon, Rob Phillips, and Ron Milo. *The Bio Mass Distribution on Earth.* PNAS. 2018 www.pnas.org/content/115/25/6506

17   Kalahari Lion Research. *Human vs Livestock vs Wild Mammal Bio Mass on Earth.* 2015 www.kalaharilionresearch.org

18   United Poultry Concerns. *Chickens Raised for Meat.* www.upc-nline.org/chickens/chickensbro.html

Chapter One

19   Online Etymology Dictionary. *Homo sapiens.*
      www.etymonline.com/word/homo%20sapiens

20   Tuttle, Russell Howard. *Human Evolution.* Encyclopaedia Britannica. 2019
      www.britannica.com/science/human-evolution

21   Wei-Haas, Maya. *Ancient Girl's Parents Were Two Different Species.*
      National Geographic. 2018. www.nationalgeographic.com/science/2018/08/
      news-denisovan-neanderthal-hominin-hybrid-ancient-human/

22   Science Daily. *Toba Catastrophe Theory.*
      www.sciencedaily.com/terms/toba_catastrophe_theory.htm

23   Wall, Jeffrey D. *Great Ape Genomics,* ILAR Journal, Is 2. 2013.
      www.academic.oup.com/ilarjournal/article/54/2/82/772507

24   Wall, Jeffrey D. *Great Ape Genomics,* ILAR Journal, Is 2. 20
      www.academic.oup.com/ilarjournal/article/54/2/82/772507

25   Wall, Jeffrey D. *Great Ape Genomics,* ILAR Journal, Is 2. 2013
      www.academic.oup.com/ilarjournal/article/54/2/82/772507

26   Wall, Jeffrey D. *Great Ape Genomics,* ILAR Journal, Is 2. 2013
      www.academic.oup.com/ilarjournal/article/54/2/82/772507

27   Worldometers. *World Population.* www.worldometers.info/world-population/

28   Worldometers. *World Population.* www.worldometers.info/world-population/

29   Dorey, Fran and Beth Blaxland. *Walking on Two Legs- Bipedalism.* Australian
      Museum. 2018 www.australianmuseum.net.au/learn/science/human-evolution/
      walking-on-two-legs-bipedalism/

30   Dorey, Fran and Beth Blaxland. Walking on Two Legs- Bipedalism. Australian
      Museum. 2018 www.australianmuseum.net.au/learn/science/human-evolution/
      walking-on-two-legs-bipedalism/

31   Dorey, Fran and Beth Blaxland. *Walking on Two Legs- Bipedalism.* Australian
      Museum. 2018 www.australianmuseum.net.au/learn/science/human-evolution/
      walking-on-two-legs-bipedalism/

32   Choi, Charles Q. *Top 10 Things That Make Humans Special.* Live Science. 2016
      www.livescience.com/15689-evolution-human-special-species.html

33   Marder, Lisa. *What Makes us Human.* ThoughtCo. 2018.
      www.thoughtco.com/what-makes-us-human-4150529

34   Marder, Lisa. *What Makes us Human.* ThoughtCo. 2018.
      www.thoughtco.com/what-makes-us-human-4150529

35   Marder, Lisa. *What Makes us Human.* ThoughtCo. 2018.
      www.thoughtco.com/what-makes-us-human-4150529

36   Choi, Charles Q. *Top 10 Things That Make Humans Special.* Live Science. 2016
      www.livescience.com/15689-evolution-human-special-species.html

37   Arbuckle, Kevin. *Why Do Women Go Through Menopause?* The Conversation. 2016. heconversation.com/why-do-women-go-through-menopause-science-offers-new-solution-to-old-puzzle-54856

38   Mukherjee, Sy. *Does Having Older Brothers Increase Men's Chances of Being Gay?* Fortune. 2017. www.fortune.com/2017/12/12/gay-genetics-older-brother-study/

39   O'Keefe, James. *Homosexuality: It's about survival-not sex.* TEDxTalks. 2016 www.youtube.com/watch?v=4Khn_z9FPmU

40   Gabbatiss, Josh. *Is Violence Embedded in our DNA?* Sapiens Anthropology / Everything Human. 2017 www.sapiens.org/evolution/human-violence-evolution/

41   Pinker, Steve. *The Blank Slate*, reprint Ed. Penguin Group USA. 2003

42   During a recent eco-tour, I had the opportunity to discuss a variety of factors involving in PTSD and returned soldiers with a psychiatrist in the field. The doctor confirmed these aspects of male aggression as contributing factors.

43   Kassube, Susanne. *Orangutan Genome*, Part 1. Orangutan Foundation International. 2014 www.orangutan.org/orangutan-genome-part-1-the-quest-for-leakeys-ancestral-great-ape/

44   Blaxland, Beth. *Humans are Apes, Great Apes.* Australian Museum. 2018 www.australianmuseum.net.au/learn/science/human-evolution/humans-are-apes-great-apes/

45   Osterath, Brigitte. *10 Facts You Probably Didn't Know About Great Apes.* DW Science. 2016 www.dw.com/en/10-facts-you-probably-didnt-know-about-great-apes/a-19189577

46   International Union for the Conservation of Nature. *Red List 2018* www.iucnredlist.org

47   Simons, Daniel. *Selective Attention Test.* YouTube. 2010. www.youtube.com/watch?v=vJG698U2Mvo

48   Chabris, Christopher and Daniel Simons. *Behind the Scenes of the Invisible Gorilla*, Blog. 2010. www.theinvisiblegorilla.com/blog/

49   This experiment has been played out in group settings and count numbers varied between both non-gorilla seeing and gorilla seeing audience members.

50   Worrall, Simon. *The Amazing Ways Your Brain Determines What You See.* National Geographic. 2017 www.news.nationalgeographic.com/2017/05/deviate-science-seeing-perception-brain-beau-lotto/

51   Chabris, Christopher and Daniel Simons. www.theinvisiblegorilla.com/overview.html

Chapter Two

52   Darwin, Charles. *On the Origin of Species*: 150th Anniversary Ed. Signet UK Reprint, 2003

53   Kuhn, Anthony. *He Helped Discover Evolution, and Then Became Extinct.* NPR Environment. 2013. www.npr.org/2013/04/30/177781424/he-helped-discover-evolution-and-then-became-extinct

54   Van Whye, John and Peter C. Kjaergaard. Abstract, *Going the Whole Orang,* Science Direct. 2015 www.sciencedirect.com/science/article/pii/S1369848615000370

55   Van Whye, John and Peter C. Kjaergaard. Abstract, *Going the Whole Orang,* Science Direct. 2015 www.sciencedirect.com/science/article/pii/S1369848615000370

56   Van Whye, John and Peter C. Kjaergaard. Abstract, *Going the Whole Orang,* Science Direct. 2015 www.sciencedirect.com/science/article/pii/S1369848615000370

57   Van Whye, John and Peter C. Kjaergaard. Abstract, *Going the Whole Orang,* Science Direct. 2015 www.sciencedirect.com/science/article/pii/S1369848615000370

58   Van Whye, John and Peter C. Kjaergaard. Abstract, *Going the Whole Orang,* Science Direct. 2015 www.sciencedirect.com/science/article/pii/S1369848615000370

59   Van Whye, John and Peter C. Kjaergaard. Abstract, *Going the Whole Orang,* Science Direct. 2015 www.sciencedirect.com/science/article/pii/S1369848615000370

60   Wallace, Alfred Russel. *The Malay Archipelago.* Penguin Classics. UK. 2014

61   Wallace, Alfred Russel. *The Malay Archipelago.* Penguin Classics. UK. 2014

62   Russon, Anne, Purwo Kuncoro, Agnes Ferisa. *Animal Creativity and Innovation, Chapter 15. Tools for the Trees.* Science Direct. 2015. www.sciencedirect.com/science/article/pii/B9780128006481000152

63   Gaines, James. *Fu Manchu Was on the Loose.* UpWorthy. 2016. www.upworthy.com/this-epic-zoo-escape-story-shows-how-fantastically-smart-orangutans-can-be

64   Harari, Yuval Noah. *Sapiens: A Brief History of Humankind.* Random House. UK 2015

65   Elena, Sanz. *Eight Striking Similarities Between Humans and Chimpanzees.* Open Mind. 2016. www.bbvaopenmind.com/en/eight-striking-similarities-between-humans-and-chimpanzees/

66   Weisberger, Mindy. *Chimps Seen Sucking Brains from Monkey's Heads.* Live Science. 2018. www.livescience.com/62288-chimps-eat-baby-monkey-brains-first.html

67   Wikipedia- The Free Encyclopedia. *Gombe Chimpanzee War.* www.en.wikipedia.org/wiki/Gombe_Chimpanzee_War

68   Ratner, Paul. *Why People Love to Hate Do-gooders Especially at Work*. Big Think. 2018. www.bigthink.com/paul-ratner/people-love-to-hate-on-do-gooders-especially-at-work?utm_medium=Social&facebook=1&utm_source=Facebook#

69   Ratner, Paul. *Why People Love to Hate Do-gooders Especially at Work*. Big Think. 2018. www.bigthink.com/paul-ratner/people-love-to-hate-on-do-gooders-especially-at-work?utm_medium=Social&facebook=1&utm_source=Facebook#

70   Parthasarathy, A. *Vedanta Treatise: The Eternities Third Ed.* Vedanta Life Institute. India 1989

Chapter Three

71   Wayman, Erin. *Six Talking Apes*. Smithsonian.com. 2011. www.smithsonianmag.com/science-nature/six-talking-apes-48085302/

72   Wayman, Erin. *Six Talking Apes*. Smithsonian.com. 2011. www.smithsonianmag.com/science-nature/six-talking-apes-48085302/

73   Fouts, Roger. *My Best friend is a Chimp*. Psychology Today. 2000. www.psychologytoday.com/us/articles/200007/my-best-friend-is-chimp

74   Wayman, Erin. *Six Talking Apes*. Smithsonian.com. 2011. www.smithsonianmag.com/science-nature/six-talking-apes-48085302/

75   Linden, Eugene. *Silent Partners: The Legacy of the Ape Language Experiments*. Ballantine Books. 1987

76   Gill, Victoria. *Orangutan Squeaks Reveal Language Evolution*. BBC News. 2017. www.bbc.com/news/science-environment-38907681

77   Berman, Robby. *Orangutans Exhibit Awareness of the Past*. Big Think. 2018. www.bigthink.com/surprising-science/orangutans-talk-past
Leif sent video and article on orang communication

78   Gill, Victoria. *Chimpanzee Language: Communication Gestures Translated*. BBC News. 2014. www.bbc.com/news/science-environment-28023630

79   Goodall, Jane. *Chimpanzee Facts*. Jane Goodall. www.janegoodall.org.uk/chimpanzees/chimpanzee-central/15-chimpanzees/chimpanzee-central/21-chimp-facts

80   Gorillas-World. *Gorilla Communication*. 2014. www.gorillas-world.com/gorilla-communication/

81   Gorillas-World. *Gorilla Communication*. 2014. www.gorillas-world.com/gorilla-communication/

82   Tzu, Sun. *The Art of War*. Shambhala Press. 2013

83   Cocks, Leif. *Orangutans My Cousins, My Friends*. The Orangutan Project. Perth WA 2016

84   Bullo, Kylie. *Reaching For the Canopy*, UWA Publishing. Perth 2015

Chapter Four

85   McLeod, Saul. *Carl Jung*. Simply Psychology. 2018.
      www.simplypsychology.org/carl-jung.html

86   McLeod, Saul. *Carl Jung*. Simply Psychology. 2018.
      www.simplypsychology.org/carl-jung.html

87   Wikipedia- The Free Encyclopedia. *The Triune Brain.*
      www.en.wikipedia.org/wiki/Triune_brain

88   Tirtha, Rama. *In Woods of God Realization.* Rama Tirtha Pratisthan; 8th edition
      (1956)

Chapter Five

89   Cherry, Kendra. *How Many Neurons Are in the Brain?* Very Well Mind. 2019.
      www.verywellmind.com/how-many-neurons-are-in-the-brain-2794889

90   Kelleher Kukolic, Siobahn. *The Average Person Has About 12,000 to 60,000
      Thoughts Per Day.* The Treasure You Seek. 2018. siobhankukolic.com/
      the-average-person-has-between-12000-and-60000-thoughts-per-day/

91   IHeartMath Institute. *Heart Brain Interactions.* The Math of Heart Math.
      2012. www.heartmath.org/articles-of-the-heart/the-math-of-heartmath/
      heart-brain-interactions/

92   Milton, John. *Paradise Lost.* Penguin Classics. London, UK. 2003.

Chapter Six

93   The story is loosely based upon a piece titled *"The Star Thrower"* by Loren Eiseley,
      first published in a book of collected essays called *"The Unexpected Universe"*
      Harvest. *1969*

94   Tafel, Rich. *Social Entrepreneurs Must Stop Throwing Starfish.* Stanford Social In-
      novation Review. 2012. www.ssir.org/articles/entry/social_entrepreneurs_must_
      stop_throwing_starfish

95   Gladwell, Malcolm, *Outliers: The story of success.* Allen Lane, Great Britain, 2008

96   Gladwell, Malcolm, *Outliers: The story of success.* Allen Lane, Great Britain, 2008

Chapter Seven

97   Wikipedia- The Free Encyclopedia. *Anthropocentrism.* en.wikipedia.org/wiki/
      Anthropocentrism

98   Boslaugh, Sarah. *Anthropocentrism.* Encyclopaedia Britannica. www.britannica.
      com/topic/anthropocentrism

99   Wikipedia- The Free Encyclopedia. *Biocentrism (ethics).* en.wikipedia.org/wiki/
      Biocentrism_(ethics)

100   DesJardins, Joseph R. *Biocentrism.* Encyclopaedia Britannica. www.britannica.
      com/topic/biocentrism

101   DesJardins, Joseph R. *Biocentrism*. Encyclopaedia Britannica. www.britannica. com/topic/biocentrism

102   Johnson, Jayme. *Biocentric Ethics and the Inherent Value of Life*. Encyclopaedia Britannica. www.britannica.com/topic/biocentrism

103   Mental Health Foundation. *Doing Good Does You Good*. www.mentalhealth.org. uk/publications/doing-good-does-you-good

104   Mental Health Foundation. *Doing Good Does You Good*. www.mentalhealth.org. uk/publications/doing-good-does-you-good

105   Anholt, Simon. The Good Country. www.goodcountry.org/

106   Anholt, Simon. The Good Country. www.goodcountry.org/

107   Anholt, Simon. Which Country Does the Most Good for the World? TED Talks. 2014. www.ted.com/talks/simon_anholt_which_country_does_the_most_good_ for_the_world

Chapter Eight

108   Wikipedia- The Free Encyclopedia. Anima and Animus. www.en.wikipedia.org/wiki/Anima_and_animus

109   Journal Psyche. *The Jungian Model of the Psyche*. www.journalpsyche.org/jungian-model-psyche/

110   Beyond the Ordinary. *Divine Balance, When Masculine Aligns with Feminine*. www.beyondtheordinaryshow.com/spiritual-dictionary/divine-balance-masculine-feminine/

111   Beyond the Ordinary. *Divine Balance, When Masculine Aligns with Feminine*. www.beyondtheordinaryshow.com/spiritual-dictionary/divine-balance-masculine-feminine/

112   Krostoski, Aleks. *Robin Dunbar: We Can Only Have 150 Friends*. The Guardian, Australia. 2010 www.theguardian.com/technology/2010/mar/14/my-bright-idea-robin-dunbar

113   University of Colorado at Boulder. *Men with Macho Faces Attractive to Fertile Women*. Science Daily. 2011

114   Barber, Nigel. *Did Stone-Age Men and Women Sleep Around and Should We Care?* Psychology Today. 2009

115   Devlin, Hannah. *Early Men and Women Were Equal, Say Scientists*. The Guardian. 2015

116   UCL Public Policy Analysis. *Where Does Social Inequality Come From? Hunter-Gatherer to Agriculture*. 2015

117   UCL Public Policy Analysis. *Where Does Social Inequality Come From? Hunter-Gatherer to Agriculture*. 2015

118   Daly, Mary. *Gyn / Ecology: The Metaethics of Radical Feminism*. Beacon Press. 1990

119   Worldometers World Population. www.worldometers.info/world-population/

120   Worldometers World Population. www.worldometers.info/world-population/

121   Food and Agriculture Organisation USA. *Agriculture and Food Security.* www.fao.org/3/x0262e/x0262e05.htm

122   DoSomething.org. *11 Facts About World Hunger.* www.dosomething.org/us/facts/11-facts-about-world-hunger

123   Boston Medical Centre. *Weight Management.* www.bmc.org/nutrition-and-weight-management/weight-management

124   Ramakrishna, Sri. *Tales and Parables of Ramakrishna.* Sri Ramakrishna Math. 2007.

Chapter Nine

125   Vocabulary.com.Dictionary. *Transcendence.* www.vocabulary.com/dictionary/transcendence

126   White, Frank. *The Overview Effect: Space Exploration and Human Evolution,* 2nd Ed. AIAA USA. 1998

127   Pinker, Steve. *The Better Angels of Our Nature: Why violence has declined.* Penguin Books. 2012

128   Pinker, Steve. *The Better Angels of Our Nature: Why violence has declined.* Penguin Books. 2012

129   Pinker, Steve. *The Better Angels of Our Nature: Why violence has declined.* Penguin Books. 2012

Epilogue

130   National Geographic. *Fireflies.* www.nationalgeographic.com/animals/invertebrates/group/fireflies/

Further Reading and Audio Visuals

Bullo, Kylie. *Reaching for the Canopy,* UWA Publishing. Perth 2015

Cocks, Leif. *Orangutans and Their Battle for Survival,* UWA Publishing. Perth 2002

Cocks, Leif. *Orangutans My Cousins, My Friends.* The Orangutan Project. Perth WA 2016

Cocks, Leif. *Orangutans My Cousins, My Friends Audio Book.* The Orangutan Project. Perth WA 2018

Darwin, Charles. *On the Origin of Species*: 150th Anniversary Ed. Signet UK Reprint, 2003

Fouts, Roger. *My Best friend is a Chimp*. Psychology Today. 2000.

Gladwell, Malcolm. *Outliers: The Story of Success.* Penguin Group. Australia 2008

Harari, Yuval Noah. *Sapiens: A Brief History of Humankind.* Random House. UK 2015

Parthasarathy, A. *Vedanta Treatise: The Eternities Third Ed.* Vedanta Life Institute. India 1989

Pinker, Steve. *The Better Angels of Our Nature: Why violence has declined.* Penguin Books. 2012

Simons, Daniel. *Selective Attention Test.* YouTube. 2010. www.youtube.com/watch?v=vJG698U2Mvo

Tirtha, Rama. *In Woods of God Realization.* Rama Tirtha Pratisthan; 8th edition (1956)

Tzu, Sun. *The Art of War.* Shambhala Press. 2013

Wallace, Alfred Russel. *The Malay Archipelago.* Penguin Classics. UK. 2014

White, Frank. *The Overview Effect: Space Exploration and Human Evolution*, 2nd Ed. AIAA USA. 1998

About the Author

For almost three decades Leif Cocks has worked tirelessly for orangutans to improve their welfare in captivity and ensure their ongoing survival in the wild. As a zoologist, author, speaker and founder of the international charity, The Orangutan Project, he is a world-renowned orangutan advocate and outspoken campaigner on their behalf.

Leif's years in the field have earned him respect within the conservation arena. He has been a key player in developing conservation plans for orangutans and influencing positive change for orangutan protection and survival. Leif is also President of the International Elephant Project, International Tiger Project and Wildlife Asia. In addition, Leif is Vice President of the Orang Utan Republik Foundation and sits on the Technical Advisory Boards of several Indonesian conservation organisations.

A small population biologist and curator by trade; Leif has several academic qualifications, including a Master of Science studying orangutans. He is a seasoned public speaker and has published several papers on orangutans in peer-reviewed journals. Leif is also the author of the books – *Orangutans and their Battle for Survival* and the Amazon Best Seller *Orangutans My Cousins, My Friends*, also published as an audio book.

Leif was a long standing Australasian Species Management Program Committee Member; a Quarantine-Approved Assessor; Zoo Husbandry Adviser; Zoo Accreditation Officer; an International Species Coordinator; and International Studbook Keeper.

He lives in Perth, Western Australia with his wife Wendy and two much loved dogs, Bonita and Shanti.

If You Would Like to Know More

For more information on how you can help support meaningful change on the ground for Critically Endangered species, visit these sites below.

The Orangutan Project
www.orangutan.org.au

International Elephant Project
www.elephant.org.au

International Tiger Project
www.tiger.org.au